500 DECORATION DETAILS: MINIMALISM

500 DÉTAILS DE DÉCORATION : MINIMALISME

500 WOHNIDEEN: MINIMALISMUS

D1529603

500 DECORATION DETAILS: MINIMALISM
500 DÉTAILS DE DÉCORATION : MINIMALISME
500 WOHNIDEEN: MINIMALISMUS

evergreen

EVERGREEN is an imprint of

TASCHEN GmbH

© 2007 TASCHEN GmbH

Hohenzollernring 53, D-50672 Köln

www.taschen.com

Editorial coordination, editor:
Simone Schleifer

Editorial assistant:
Macarena San Martín, Esther Moreno

Text:
Simone Schleifer, Daniela Santos Quartino

English translation:
Gene Ferber

French translation:
Marion Westerhoff

German translation:
Susanne Engler

Proofreading:
Bridget Vranckx, Cecile Cano, Martin Rolshoven

Art director:
Mireia Casanovas Soley

Graphic design and layout:
Oriol Serra Juncosa, Laura Millán

Printed in Spain

ISBN 978-3-8365-0098-2

Contents Sommaire Inhalt

More than forty years after its first appearance as an artistic movement, minimalism is one of the most enduring trends of our times and a solidly established esthetic aspect of architecture and design. Living spaces that follow the parameters established by this movement possess a contemporary quality that is both youthful and avant-garde despite their apparent formality. Various theories have been put forward about the origins of minimalism. Some consider it a perfected version of rationalism and abstraction that grew out of the rise of industry towards the end of the 19th century. Others see in it as Eastern influence and, more specifically, the influence of Japanese culture and architecture.

Some aspects of minimalism first appeared in architecture with Le Corbusier and with the Bauhaus School of Art and Design whose director, Ludwig Mies Van der Rohe, is considered to be the movement's spiritual father. His well-known dictums 'less is more' and 'God is in the details' gave shape to the rules that would come to govern minimalism.

The term 'minimalist', however, was coined in the 1960s by critics who were trying to give a name to the predominant movement in the visual arts. Minimalism reached its maturity a decade later, imposing itself as a reaction against pop art, which was saturating the media at the time. Since then the influence of this movement has transcended the fields of design and architecture and entered the realm of painting, fashion, and music. In interior design, minimalism can be defined by the following characteristics: simple forms, pure lines, unobstructed spaces and neutral colors. This style advocates harmonious as well as functional surroundings, and banishes excesses or any kind of visual 'pollution'. Despite the strictness of its principles, the increasing popularity of minimalism has toned down the rules a little in order to create more livable and less strict, and ultimately more human, domestic environments. This book offers decoration ideas based on the most contemporary form of minimalism, as well as inspiring maxims of the leading exponents of this movement.

Plus de quarante ans après son apparition en tant que phénomène artistique, le minimalisme, un des courants actuels les plus stables, s'est affirmé comme étant une expression esthétique de l'architecture et du design. Les espaces de vie conçus selon les critères de ce courant, revêtent des allures contemporaines qui, malgré le formalisme des principes appliqués, sont également empreintes de jeunesse et d'avant-garde.

On a tissé diverses théories sur les origines du minimalisme. Certains d'estimer que c'est une version perfectionnée du rationalisme et de l'abstraction favorisée par l'essor de l'industrie de la fin du XIXe siècle. D'autres de voir dans le minimalisme l'influence de la culture orientale, et, plus exactement, de l'architecture japonaise.

Les premières règles concrètes surgissent avec l'architecture de Le Corbusier et de Ludwig Mies Van der Rohe, directeur de l'Ecole de l'Art et du Design du Bauhaus, considéré comme étant le père spirituel de ce courant. À travers ses fameux énoncés « moins est plus » et « Dieu est dans les détails », il a forgé les principes qui régiront le minimalisme.

Mais ce n'est que dans les années soixante que la critique crée le terme « minimaliste », désignant ainsi le mouvement qui s'impose alors dans les arts visuels. Il faut attendre une décennie pour que le minimalisme atteigne sa maturité, se présentant comme une réaction à l'art pop et à la saturation des contenus des moyens de communication. Depuis lors, son influence s'est étendue bien au-delà des domaines du design et de l'architecture, pour atteindre la peinture, la mode et la musique.

Dans l'architecture d'intérieur, le minimalisme se définit par les caractéristiques suivantes : simplicité des formes, lignes épurées, espaces dépouillés et couleurs neutres. Ce style prône les univers harmonieux et fonctionnels, bannissant l'excès et toute pollution visuelle. Malgré la grande rigueur de ses principes, le minimalisme, face à sa popularité croissante, a dû les nuancer pour créer des espaces de vie plus habitables et moins stricts, finalement plus humains. Le présent ouvrage réunit des propositions de décoration qui affichent une nouvelle version plus contemporaine du minimalisme, les agrémentant de phrases inspiratrices des plus éminents représentants de ce mouvement.

Über vierzig Jahre nach seinem ersten Auftreten als künstlerische Ausdrucksform ist der Minimalismus eine der stabilsten Strömungen der heutigen Zeit und hat sich zu einer der grundlegenden Stilrichtungen in der Architektur und Raumgestaltung entwickelt. Die nach den Parametern dieser Stilrichtung entworfenen Wohnumgebungen wirken sehr zeitgemäß und trotz der Anwendung sehr formeller Grundsätze auch jugendlich und avantgardistisch.

Es gibt verschiedene Theorien über den Ursprung des Minimalismus. Manche betrachten ihn als eine perfektionierte Version des Rationalismus und der Abstraktion, die durch den industriellen Aufschwung gegen Ende des 19. Jahrhunderts gefördert wurde. Andere wiederum glauben im Minimalismus den Einfluss der östlichen Kultur, genauer gesagt, der japanischen Architektur zu erkennen.

Die ersten konkreten Richtlinien in der Architektur entstanden durch die Arbeit von Le Corbusier und dem Leiter der Schule für Kunst und Gestaltung Bauhaus, Ludwig Mies van der Rohe, der als der spirituelle Vater dieser Strömung betrachtet wird. Er gab den Normen, die den Minimalismus bestimmen, durch seine berühmten Leitsätze, wie „wenig ist mehr" und „Gott ist im Detail", seine Form.

Es war jedoch in den Sechzigerjahren, als die Kritik den Begriff „minimalistisch" prägte, um damit eine Bewegung zu bezeichnen, die sich in dieser Zeit in den visuellen Künsten durchsetzte. Ein Jahrzehnt später erreichte der Minimalismus seine Reife und stellte eine Art Reaktion auf die Pop-Art und die Übersättigung der Kommunikationsmittel mit Inhalten dar. Seitdem ist der Einfluss dieser Bewegung weit über die Gestaltung und Architektur hinausgegangen und hat die Malerei, die Mode und die Musik erfasst.

Die Charakteristika, die den Minimalismus definieren, sind im Bereich der Innenarchitektur die Einfachheit der Formen, die reinen Linien, die leeren Räume und die neutralen Farben. Dieser Stil setzt auf harmonische und funktionelle Umgebungen und verzichtet auf jede Art von Übermaß, insbesondere im visuellen Bereich. Obwohl diese Grundsätze im Wesentlichen weiterhin gültig sind, hat die Popularität des Minimalismus gleichzeitig dazu geführt, dass die strengen Regeln abgeschwächt wurden, um die Räume für den modernen Menschen angenehm zu gestalten. Der vorliegende Band zeigt Möglichkeiten der Raumgestaltung, die eine moderne Variante des Minimalismus zeigen. Zitate der wichtigsten Vertreter dieser Bewegung sollen dem Leser dabei als inspirierende Quelle dienen.

500 DECORATION DETAILS: MINIMALISM
500 DÉTAILS DE DÉCORATION : MINIMALISME
500 WOHNIDEEN: MINIMALISMUS

Storage

Rangement

Aufbewahrung

One of the basic rules of minimalism is to achieve maximum effect with the smallest number of components. For this reason shelves and storage furniture play a vital role in helping to avoid the effect of untidiness that usually results from the accumulation of objects. It is a matter of distributing space into well-defined geometric compartments that will clearly mark out the various storage areas. For this purpose square or rectangular-shaped pieces of furniture offer a better storage capacity, as well as a neat and light appearance. Compact, modular volumes can then contribute to the purity of lines advocated by this esthetic movement. If one is to follow the most dogmatic school of minimalism and get close to abstraction, the best choice is simple materials, smooth, flat surfaces, and similar colors or complementary to those dominant in the space to be furnished.

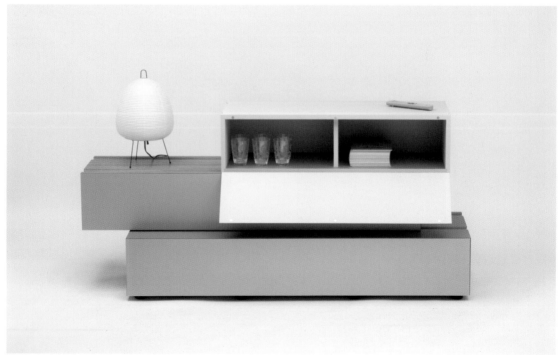

Performa

Un des principes du minimalisme est d'obtenir un résultat optimal avec le moins d'éléments possibles. Pour ce faire, étagères et meubles de rangement jouent un rôle essentiel pour éviter le foisonnement d'objets et le sentiment de désordre qui en découle. Il s'agit, en définitive, de distribuer l'espace en sections aux lignes géométriques très définies, délimitant clairement les zones de rangement. Dans ce sens, les meubles aux formes carrées ou rectangulaires offrent une plus grande capacité de rangement, affichant des lignes épurées et claires. De même, les volumes compacts et modulaires s'inscrivent dans la pureté des lignes, propre à ce courant esthétique. Pour tendre vers l'abstraction, on utilise des matériaux simples, les surfaces sont lisses et planes, les couleurs identiques à celles qui prédominent dans les espaces de vie – selon la version plus dogmatique – ou bien complémentaires.

Einer der Grundsätze des Minimalismus ist es, eine zufrieden stellende Wirkung mit so wenig Komponenten wie möglich zu erzielen. Dabei spielen Regale und Möbelstücke zum Lagern eine wichtige Rolle. Sie verhindern, dass sich Objekte anhäufen und so den Eindruck von Unordnung entstehen lassen. Ziel ist es, den Raum in Bereiche mit genau definierten, geometrischen Linien aufzuteilen, die deutlich die Lagerbereiche begrenzen. Möbel mit quadratischen und rechteckigen Formen haben eine größere Lagerkapazität und wirken deshalb klarer und leichter. Ebenso passen kompakte und modulare Formen gut zur Reinheit der Linien dieser ästhetischen Strömung. Um der Abstraktion nahe zu kommen, werden einfache Materialien verwendet, und die Flächen sind glatt und flach. Wenn man sich streng an die stilistischen Regeln hält, haben diese Möbel die gleichen Farben wie der Raum, und wenn man sich etwas mehr Freiheit erlaubt, sind Komplementärfarben zulässig.

Orange 22

Bonaldo

Nils Holger Moormann

ils Holger Moormann

A metal sheet, mounted horizontally or vertically on the wall, can provide many storage possibilities as the boxes are held in position magnetically.
Une feuille de métal, montée à l'horizontale ou la verticale sur le mur, offre de nombreuses possibilités de rangement, car les boites se fixent magnétiquement dans n'importe qu'elle position.
Ein Metallblech, horizontal oder vertikal an die Wand montiert, bietet zahlreiche Lagermöglichkeiten in den Kästen, die magnetisch daran befestigt werden.

Nils Holger Moormann

LUKAS   MAX   CECILIA   FRANK

Nils Holger Moormar

More than just a wardrobe, this is also a key-holder, mirror, memo-board and children's coat rack all in one system, which provides extra storage space for everyday accessories and at the same time simplifies and organizes the entrance area.

Plus qu'une simple armoire – elle est à la fois porte-clé, miroir, panneau pense-bête et aussi portemanteau pour enfants : tous réunis en un seul système, sans oublier l'espace de rangement d'appoint pour les accessoires quotidiens, créé pour simplifier et organiser la zone d'entrée.

Das ist nicht einfach nur eine Garderobe, sondern es kann ein Schlüsselhalter, ein Spiegel, eine Pinnwand oder ein Garderobenständer für Kinder hinzugefügt werden: so wird nicht nur zusätzlicher Lagerraum für die alltäglichen Dinge gewonnen, es dient auch um den Eingangsbereich zu organisieren und übersichtlicher zu gestalten.

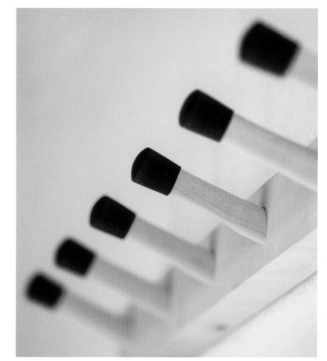

Nils Holger Moormann

Nils Holger Moormar

This light, graceful and handy writing stand can be placed against almost any wall or shelf, offering a surface space that is large enough for a telephone, for example, or for jotting something down.

Cette écritoire sur pied légère, gracieuse et pratique peut être presque placée contre n'importe quel mur ou étagère, offrant une surface assez grande pour y mettre un téléphone, par exemple, ou pour y déposer un objet.

Dieser leichte, anmutige und praktische Schreibständer kann an fast jede Wand oder jedes Regal gelehnt werden. Die Fläche ist groß genug, um ein Telefon darauf zu stellen und um etwas zu notieren.

Nils Holger Moormann

Nils Holger Moormann

Amor de Madre

A great number of books can be neatly displayed in this space-saving, freestanding rack that is easily assembled and can be extended upward if necessary.

Un grand nombre de livres peut être soigneusement rangé sur cette étagère sur pied, facile à assembler et rallonger en hauteur si nécessaire.

Auf diesem frei stehenden und raumsparenden Regal können viele Bücher übersichtlich angeordnet werden. Es kann einfach aufgebaut und nach oben erweitert werden.

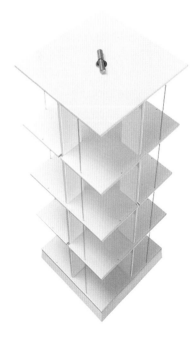

Nils Holger Moormann

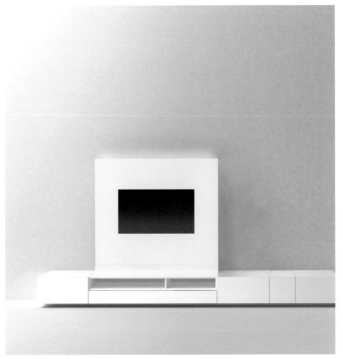

Pallucco

"It seems justified to affirm: the more cultivated a people becomes, the more decoration disappears."
Le Corbusier

« Il semble justifié d'affirmer que plus la personne est cultivée, plus la décoration se fait rare. »
Le Corbusier

„Man kann wohl bekräftigen, dass, umso kultivierter die Menschen werden, umso mehr Dekoration verschwindet."
Le Corbusier

ls Holger Moormann

Thanks to its lightness this table, in birch veneer, can be folded and stored away easily.
Grâce à sa légèreté, cette table, en bouleau verni, est pliable et facilement stockable.
Dieser leichte Tisch mit Birkenfurnier kann zusammengeklappt und einfach verstaut werden.

La Maison de Marin

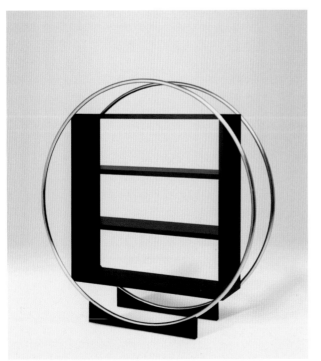

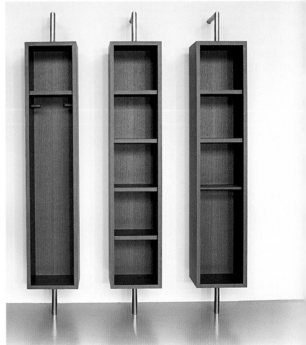

Armani Casa

Toscoquattr

Nils Holger Moorman

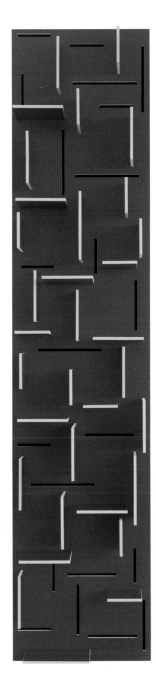

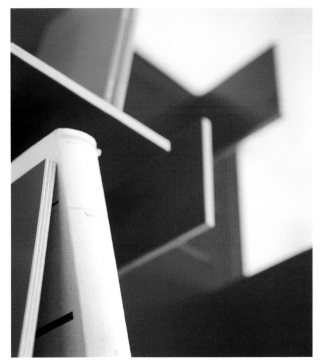

Nils Holger Moormann

Trays are randomly inserted into a wall panel, so that each shelf system has its own unique look. This shelf provides an attractive place not just for books, but also for anything else that requires a special place on the wall.

La structure est intégrée à un panneau mural, octroyant ainsi à chaque système d'étagères un caractère unique. Ces étagères sont un emplacement idéal pour les livres mais aussi pour tout élément à mettre en valeur sur le mur.

In ein Wandpaneel werden Tablare in beliebiger Anordnung hineingesteckt, so dass sich für jedes Regal ein eigenes Bild ergibt. In diesen Regalen sind nicht nur Bücher gut aufgehoben, sondern auch alle anderen Dinge, die einen besonderen Platz an der Wand beanspruchen.

"Design can be art. Design can be aesthetics.
Design is so simple, that's why it is so
complicated."
Paul Rand

« Le design peut être art. Le design peut être
esthétique. Le design n'est pas simple, c'est
pourquoi il est si compliqué. »
Paul Rand

„Design kann Kunst sein. Design kann Ästhetik
sein. Design ist so einfach, deshalb ist es so
kompliziert."
Paul Rand

1 Nils Holger Moormann 2 La Maison de Marina 3, 4, 7 Galería Joan Gaspar 5 Desu Design 6 Armani Cas

Lighting

Éclairage

Beleuchtung

Minimalist environments convey peace and tranquility. Simple lighting is crucial for creating or enhancing an ethereal atmosphere, and the sources of light, going beyond mere functionality, become implicit visual elements in the configuration of these environments. It is recommended to use unadorned shapes, stripped of any kind of artifact, such as clean geometrical volumes, pure colors, spherical or cubic lampshades, and supports made of metal or natural materials. The light in minimalist surroundings should be intense and therefore belong to the range of cool colors that help formulate the kind of bold environments in which concealment or camouflage is impossible. Placed strategically, the sources of light are a useful tool for bringing out the pure lines of the furniture and decorative details.

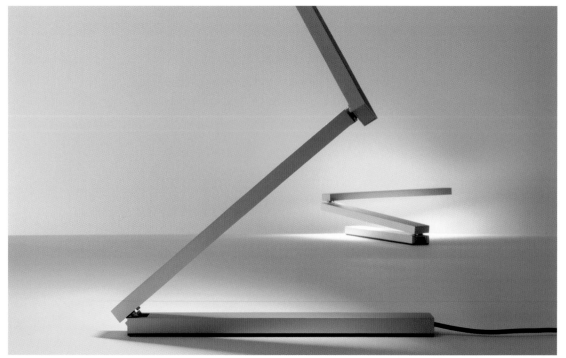

Biosca & Botey

Les univers minimalistes dégagent calme et paix. Ce phénomène est le fruit d'une atmosphère éthérée mise en scène par un éclairage simple, dont la présence est décisive. Dans ce contexte, au-delà de la fonction, l'aspect formel des sources de lumière est essentiel à la configuration de ces espaces. Pour ce faire, la préférence va aux formes sobres et dépouillées de tout artifice : volumes géométriques aux lignes épurées et couleurs pures, écrans sphériques ou cubiques et supports en métal ou matériaux naturels. La lumière des espaces minimalistes est intense et se situe dans la gamme des couleurs froides, génératrices d'ambiances immaculées où l'on ne peut rien cacher ni camoufler. Les sources de lumière, véritables ustensiles, sont situées à des points stratégiques, pour exalter les lignes des meubles et les détails décoratifs.

Minimalistische Wohnumgebungen vermitteln Ruhe und Frieden. Diese Wirkung ist das Ergebnis einer schwerelosen Umgebung, unterstrichen durch eine einfache Beleuchtung, die jedoch entscheidend den Raum prägt. Deshalb dienen die verschiedenen Lichtquellen nicht nur der Beleuchtung, sondern sie bilden ein entscheidendes Element in der Gestaltung minimalistischer Wohnumgebungen. Bevorzugt werden schlichte Lampen ohne überflüssigen Tand. Es können Lampen mit geometrischen Formen und einem einfachen Aussehen und reinen Farben gewählt werden, oder auch kugel- oder würfelförmige Schirme, Metallträger oder Lampen aus Naturmaterialien. Das Licht in minimalistisch gestalteten Räumen ist intensiv und hat eine kalte Farbe. Durch diese Art von Beleuchtung entstehen Umgebungen, in denen nichts verborgen oder getarnt wird. Die Lichtquellen dienen als Werkzeug, das an strategischen Stellen die reinen Linien der Möbel und die dekorativen Details unterstreicht.

Santa & Cole

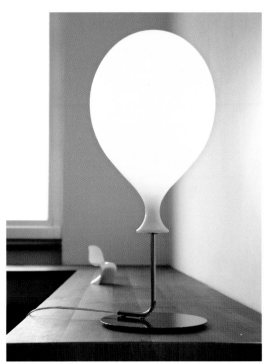

Büro für Form

Julian Appelius | © Andreas Velten

Intended as a bedside lamp, this curved, powder-coated metal sheet can hang on the left or the right of the bed. Mounted on the wall, it serves both as a lamp and a bedside table. The pre-assembled light fitting just slots in.

Prévue pour être une lampe de chevet, cette feuille de métal incurvée et poudrée peut être accrochée, soit à gauche soit à droite du lit, même au mur, et sert à la fois de lampe et de table de chevet. La lumière déjà assemblée s'insère dans la fente.

Dieses gekrümmte, pulverbeschichtete Metallblech ist eigentlich als Tischlampe für das Schlafzimmer gedacht. Man kann es entweder rechts oder links vom Bett aufhängen oder an die Wand montieren, und es dient gleichzeitig als Nachttischchen und Lampe. Die vormontierte Lampe wird einfach in die Kerbe eingesteckt.

Julian Appelius | © Thomas Koy

Julian Appelius | © Thomas Koy

Büro für Form

Büro für Form

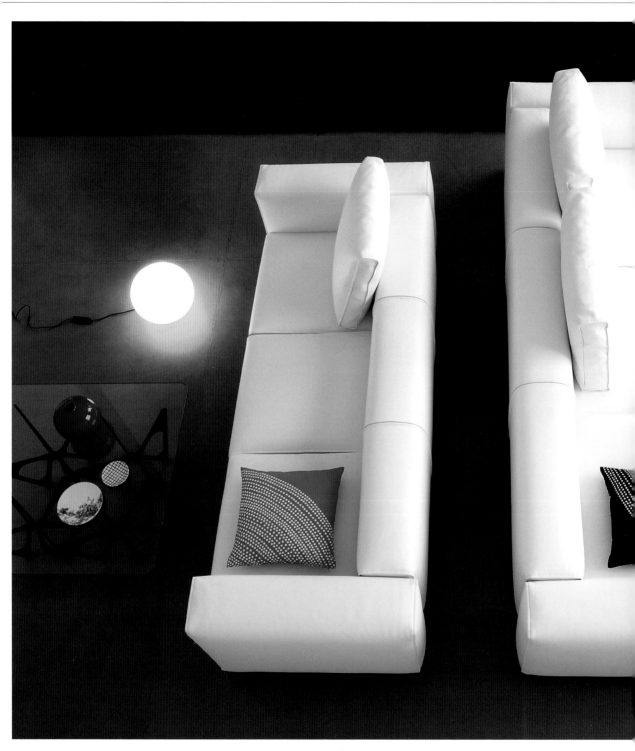

The Dutch design duo Stefan Scholten and Carole Baijings exhibited their new lighting system, Light Ball, for the first time at the Salone Internazionale in Milan. Transparency, texture and the choice of soft colors are key elements of their design.

Le duo de designers hollandais, le Stefan Scholten et Carole Baijings, expose son nouveau système d'éclairage, Light Ball, pour la première fois au « Salone Internazionale de Milan. » Transparence, texture et sélection de couleurs douces sont les éléments clé de leur design.

Die holländischen Designer Stefan Scholten und Carole Baijings stellten ihr neues Beleuchtungssystem „Light Ball" zum ersten Mal während des „Salone Internazionale" in Mailand aus. Transparenz, Textur und die sanften Farben sind die Schlüsselelemente ihres Entwurfes.

"Make everything as simple as possible, but not simpler."
Albert Einstein

« Faites tout aussi simple que possible mais pas plus simple. »
Albert Einstein

„Mach alles so einfach wie möglich, aber nicht einfacher."
Albert Einstein

1, 5 Droog 2, 4, 6 Armani Casa 3 Büro für Form 7 Marse

Galería Joan Gaspar

Armani Casa

A totally contemporary look created by Armani Casa for a table lamp that reflects Asian esthetics. The warm emotive color is not used in contrast to the simple minimalist shape, but rather in harmonious juxtaposition.

Une allure totalement contemporaine créée par Armani Casa pour une lampe de table reflétant l'esthétique asiatique. Les chaudes couleurs sensuelles ne sont pas utilisées comme contraste à la simple forme minimaliste, mais plutôt pour créer d'harmonieuses juxtapositions.

Ein völlig zeitgemäßer Look, der von Armani Casa für eine Tischlampe in asiatischer Optik entworfen wurde. Die warme und gefühlvolle Farbe wird nicht als Kontrast zu der minimalistischen Form, sondern als eine Art Nebeneinanderstellung benutzt.

Armani Casa

Büro für For

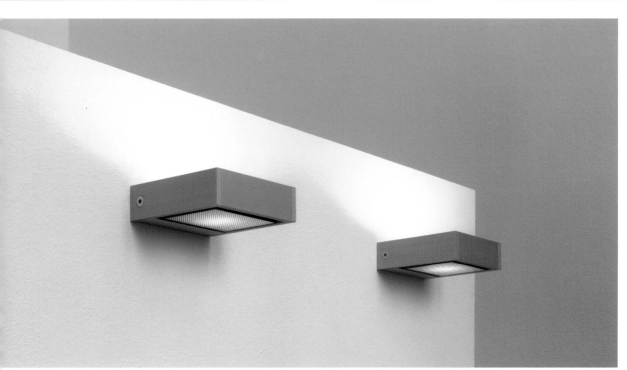

osca & Botey

osca & Botey

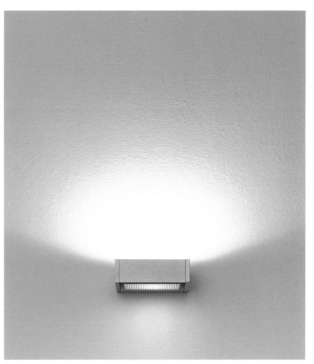

Biosca & Botey

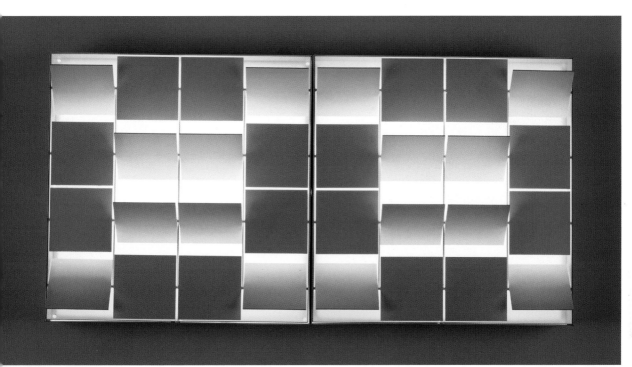

Santa & Cole

Marset

Santa & Cole

Zanott

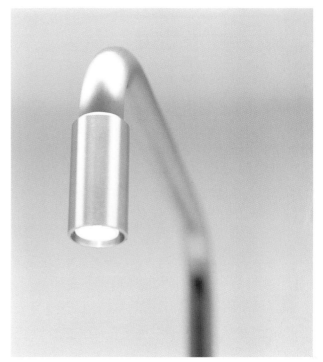

Shin Azumi

The dimmer of this lighting system is shaped like a shower tap, suggesting an obvious and delicate way of controlling the amount of light needed. This design is not only functional, it also stirs the imagination as the light seems to flow and bathe the room like water pouring out of a showerhead.

L'interrupteur du tamiseur de ce système d'éclairage a la forme d'un pommeau de douche, suggérant une manière subtile et délicate de contrôler la quantité de lumière nécessaire. Ce design n'est pas fonctionnel : il fait appel à l'imagination puisque la lumière semble couler et inonder la pièce, à l'instar de l'eau diffusée par une tête de douche.

Der Dimmerschalter dieses Lichtsystems hat die Form einer Duscharmatur; eine Anspielung darauf, dass man mit diesem Schalter ganz offensichtlich und sehr genau die notwendige Lichtmenge einstellen kann. Dieses Design ist nicht nur funktionell, sondern es regt auch die Phantasie an, in der das Licht in den Raum fließt, so wie Wasser aus dem Duschkopf strömt, und der Raum in Licht gebadet wird.

Studio decoration

Décoration de studio

Studio-Dekoration

Thanks to its stark shapes and rational organization of space, minimalism provides the serenity required in working areas. As this esthetic trend also aims to create spaciousness, the decoration dispenses with any object that may impede movement or cause distraction. For this reason, the preferred type of furniture and accessories are those that perform specific functions and, more importantly, maintain a sense of order. Light supporting towers, office furniture, desk protectors, filing cabinets and boxes can all become interesting items of decoration in their own right as long as they show a unity of texture and tone. As for lighting, this is austere and directed towards the working area. Architecturally-inspired lamps are particularly effective as they provide an excellent quality of light while adding a contemporary, sober and elegant touch.

Müller

Fort des ses formes essentielles et d'une distribution rationnelle de l'espace, le minimalisme dégage une sérénité propice aux aires de travail. L'objectif de ce courant étant de privilégier les espaces amples, la décoration se passe de tout objet susceptible d'entraver les mouvements et distraire l'attention. Pour ce faire, les meubles et accessoires utilisés sont certes choisis pour leurs fonctions spécifiques, mais avant tout, parce qu'ils sont générateurs d'ordre. Ainsi, colonnes de support ultra légères, matériel de bureau, boites porte-documents, classeurs et protège- bureau se transforment en éléments décoratifs, dès qu'ils affichent une unité de texture et de ton. L'éclairage, pour sa part, sera austère et dirigé ponctuellement sur l'aire de travail. Les lampes d'inspiration architecturale sont efficaces grâce à la lumière optimale qu'elles diffusent, tout en affichant un air contemporain, élégant et sobre.

Aufgrund der einfachen Formen und der rationalen Raumaufteilung sorgt der minimalistische Stil für die Klarheit, die in Arbeitsbereichen notwendig ist. Da es das erklärte Ziel dieser ästhetischen Strömung ist, die Räume groß und weit wirken zu lassen, verzichtet man bei der Dekoration auf alle Objekte, die die freie Bewegung behindern oder die Aufmerksamkeit ablenken könnten. Deshalb werden Möbel und Gegenstände verwendet, die spezifische Funktionen erfüllen, und die vor allem für Ordnung sorgen. So werden die Computertürme mit leichten Halterungen, das Büromaterial, die Dokumentenkästen, die Aktenordner und die Schreibtischschoner zu dekorativen Blickpunkten, solange sie in Textur und Farbe einheitlich sind. Die Beleuchtung wiederum sollte nüchtern und auf den Arbeitsbereich gerichtet sein. Die von der Architektur inspirierten Lampen strahlen ein Licht hochwertiger Qualität aus und wirken modern, elegant und schlicht. Sie passen ausgezeichnet in diese Bereiche.

Müller

Müller

Joseph Graceffa & Dario Buzzi

The construction principle on which this series is based lends itself perfectly to a classic accessory like this Magazine holder. Designed by the Campana brothers for Alessi, it is part of a series of aluminum wire products, made of random steel rods welded together.

Le principe de construction, base de cette série, s'adapte parfaitement à un accessoire comme ce porte magazine. Conçu par les frères Campana Alessi, il fait partie d'une série de produits à base de fils d'aluminium, assemblés au hasard.

Das Konstruktionsprinzip, auf dem diese Serie basiert, eignet sich perfekt für ein klassisches Accessoire wie einen Zeitschriftenständer. Dieses, von den Campana Brothers für Alessi entworfene, Element ist Teil einer Serie von Produkten aus Aluminiumdraht, hergestellt aus zusammengeschweißten Stahlstäbchen.

Alessi

Balvi

Muji

ellato

Bellato

This workstation unit meets all the demands of work, allowing possible
additions while taking up minimum space. The moveable shelves come
in different sizes to accommodate a desktop computer, a video screen
and a printer. A special container holds the tower, CDs, paper and
documents.

Ce set de poste de travail répond à toutes les exigences du travail,
permettant également d'ajouter des éléments pour un minimum de
place. Les étagères amovibles sont de différentes tailles pour s'adapter
à un bureau d'ordinateur, un écran de vidéo et une imprimante. Un
container contient la tour, les CD, le papier et les documents.

Diese Arbeitsplatzeinheit entspricht allen Anforderungen, nimmt nur
minimal Platz ein und kann erweitert werden. Die verschiebbaren
Regale werden in verschiedenen Größen geliefert, so dass ein
Computer, ein Bildschirm und ein Drucker darauf passen. In einem
speziellen Fach sind der Turm, die CDs, Papier und Dokumente
untergebracht.

Bellato

The Alessi Pens, created by the Egyptian-American architect Hani Rashid, belong to a range of desktop items that challenge the design of everyday office items. They have been developed in collaboration with Mitsubishi Pencil, the Japanese experts of writing instruments.

Les crayons Alessi, créés par l'architecte égypto américain Hani Rashid, s'inscrivent dans une panoplie d'articles de bureaux, qui relève le design des articles habituels. Ils sont développés en collaboration avec Mitsubishi Pencil, les experts japonais en instruments d'écriture.

Die, von dem ägyptisch-amerikanischen Architekten Hani Rashid entworfenen, Alessi Pens gehören zu einem Sortiment von Schreibtischutensilien, dessen alltägliche Büroobjekte sich durch ihr erstaunliches Design auszeichnen. Sie wurden in Zusammenarbeit mit Mitsubishi Pencil, den japanischen Experten für Schreibgeräte, entworfen.

Alessi

Balvi

Balvi

Vitr

Vitra

Bellato

Bella

Bellato

Highly individual, this compact desk made of gray lacquered steel includes a drawer, space for CD and paper storage and a rear cable outlet. The design is both simple and contemporary.

Hautement individuel, ce bureau compact comprend un tiroir, des CD et de l'espace pour ranger les papiers, ainsi qu'une sortie de câble enroulable. Réalisé en acier laqué gris, son design est à la fois simple et contemporain.

Dieser kompakte, sehr individuelle Schreibtisch ist mit einer Schublade, Fächern zum Aufbewahren von CDs und Papier sowie einem hinteren Kabelausgang ausgestattet. Das Design dieses Tisches aus grau lackiertem Stahl ist einfach und zeitgemäß.

Formal rigor, technological research and impeccable execution characterize the design of this unique collection. A specific range of accessories is incorporated for a truly functional desk.
Rigueur formelle, recherche technologique et exécution parfaite caractérisent le design de cette collection unique. Un éventail particulier d'accessoires est intégré pour un bureau fonctionnel.
Die formelle Strenge, technologische Analyse und eine einwandfreie Ausführung charakterisieren das Design dieser einzigartigen Kollektion. Eine spezifische Auswahl an Zubehör wurde darin aufgenommen; Elemente, mit denen man den Schreibtisch wirklich funktionell organisiert.

Desalto

Desalto

:ra

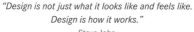

"Design is not just what it looks like and feels like. Design is how it works."
Steve Jobs

« Le design ce n'est pas uniquement son apparence et les sentiments qu'il dégage. Le design, c'est savoir comment il fonctionne ».
Steve Jobs

„Design ist nicht nur, wie es aussieht und wie es sich anfühlt. Design ist, wie es funktioniert."
Steve Jobs

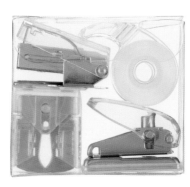

1, 2, 4, 5, 6 Muji 3 Performa 7 La Maison de Mari

Molteni & C

Kitchen decoration

Décoration de cuisine

Küchen-Dekoration

Clean, wide work surfaces give minimalist kitchens a kind of functional estheticism that aims to make the most of space and allow maximum freedom of movement. In such surroundings heavy hanging objects and other decorative artifacts should be avoided, and cool, discreet lighting is recommended for food-handling areas. Utensils and small kitchen appliances should be kept out of sight, in compact cupboards of pure colors, and cooking ingredients should be stored in identical containers. As for tableware, cutlery and glassware, they should all be plain with strong pure lines. White is the color traditionally associated with minimalism, but a more lenient version of this esthetic movement will accept other colors as long as they are pure. The combination of ceramic or porcelain and stainless steel is one of the best ways of achieving this style.

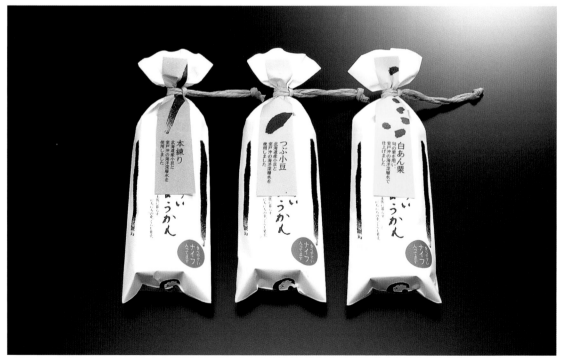

Matusaki

Avec leurs surfaces immaculées et spacieuses, les cuisines minimalistes tendent à afficher une esthétique fonctionnelle, visant tant
à la maximalisation de l'espace qu'à la configuration de larges
zones de circulation. Dans cet univers, les tirants chargés et autres
accessoires décoratifs sont superflus. De même, l'éclairage se fait
discret et se décline en teintes froides pour les zones de manipula-
tion des aliments. Les ustensiles et les petits appareils électromé-
nagers, restent, pour leur part, hors de vue, disparaissant dans des
armoires aux formes compactes et aux couleurs pures. Les ingrédients culinaires sont rangés dans des pots de même apparence. Il
en va de même pour la vaisselle, les couverts et la verrerie qui,
dépourvus d'ornementation, affichent une évidente pureté formelle.
Traditionnellement, le minimalisme est associé au blanc, mais dans
une version moins puriste, les couleurs sont admises à condition
d'être toujours pures. Dans ce sens, la céramique et la porcelaine,
aux côtés de l'acier inoxydable, sont une des associations les plus
heureuses pour parachever ce style.

Minimalistisch gestaltete Küchen zeichnen sich durch eine funktionelle Ästhetik aus, in der zum einen der Platz optimal ausgenutzt
wird und zum anderen weite Durchgangsbereiche entstehen. In
einer solchen Umgebung sind überladene Träger und anderer,
dekorativer Tand überflüssig. Die Beleuchtung in den Bereichen, in
denen die Lebensmittel zubereitet werden, sollte zurückhaltend
sein und eine kalte Farbe haben. Das Küchenzubehör und die kleinen Haushaltsgeräte werden in kompakten Schränken in reinen
Farben aufbewahrt, so dass sie außer Sichtweite sind. Lebensmittel werden in ähnlichen Schränken oder Kästen gelagert. Auch das
Geschirr, das Besteck und die Gläser sollten schlicht und
schmucklos sein und sich vor allem durch die Reinheit ihrer Formen auszeichnen. Traditionell assoziiert man mit dem Minimalismus die Farbe Weiß, aber in einer weniger dogmatischen Version
werden auch andere Farben akzeptiert. Es sollte sich jedoch stets
um reine Farben handeln. Deshalb eignet sich die Kombination von
Keramik und Porzellan mit Edelstahl ausgezeichnet für diese Stilrichtung.

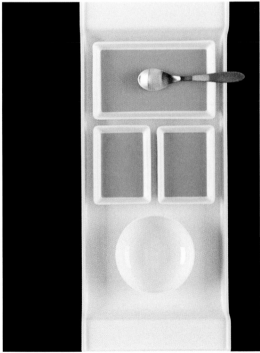

Rörstrand

Enric Rovira

The unglazed yet water-resistant ceramic gives the Tea & Sake sets a typical dark matt color. The lid fits neatly in the body and a strip of mesh is fitted inside to strain the tea while still in the pot, thus helping the leaves keep their freshness.

La céramique brute mais résistante à l'eau de ce set de Tea & Sake, lui confère une couleur mate typique. Le couvercle s'adapte au pot avec un jeu minimum, et un filet est placé à l'intérieur pour verser le thé alors qu'il est encore dans le pot, pour que les feuilles gardent leur fraîcheur.

Die unlasierte, aber dennoch wasserbeständige Keramik verleiht diesem Tee & Sake Set seine typische dunkle, matte Farbe. Der Deckel passt sehr genau auf die Kanne, in der sich ein Teenetz befindet, sodass der Tee darin selbst ziehen kann und die Teeblätter ihre Frische bewahren.

Shin Azumi

n Azumi

Shin Azumi

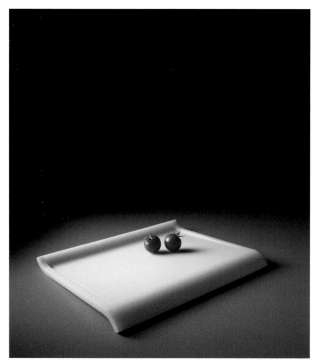

Dedece

This chopping board breaks away from more conventional ones thanks to its tilted angle that enables liquids to run into a small collector from which they can be poured easily. The material is easy to handle and maintain.

Cette planche à découper sort des sentiers battus grâce à son angle incliné qui permet au liquide de couler dans un petit récipient pour le verser facilement ensuite. Le matériel est facile à manipuler et entretenir.

Diese Schneidbretter unterscheiden sich von den konventionellen durch eine schräge Kante, über die Flüssigkeiten in einen kleinen Auffangbehälter laufen, der leicht entleert werden kann. Das Material ist einfach zu benutzen und zu pflegen.

Ale

Georg Jensen

Spices and other cooking ingredients are no longer tucked away out of sight in closed cupboards. They now proudly take their place in decorative containers, such as these stainless-steel salt and pepper mills designed by Philip Bro Ludvigsen.

Autrefois les épices et autres ingrédients ne se gardaient pas dans des armoires fermées mais dans des récipients décoratifs visibles comme le sont, par exemple, les moulins à sel et poivre en acier inoxydables signés Philip Bro Ludvigsen.

Schon lange hebt man Gewürze und andere Zutaten nicht mehr in geschlossenen Schränken, sondern in gut sichtbaren, dekorativen Behältern auf. Ein Beispiel dafür sind die Pfeffer- und Salzmühlen aus Edelstahl von Philip Bro Ludvigsen.

Alessi

Alessi

© Jordi Miralles

"The more minimal the art, the more maximum
the explanation."
Hilton Kramer

« Plus l'art est minimal, plus il faut l'expliquer. »
Hilton Kramer

„Je minimaler die Kunst ist, umso größer ist die
Erklärung."
Hilton Kramer

Schiffir

1

2

3

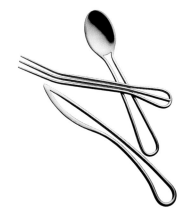

4

"The suppression of decoration is necessary to regulate passion."
Adolf Loos

« Il faut supprimer le décor pour réguler la passion. »
Adolf Loos

„Die Abschaffung des Ornaments ist notwendig, um die Leidenschaft zu lenken."
Adolf Loos

Broccoli
Pasta
Chili

5

6

7

6

1 Form Fresh | © Marcel Crist **2** El Bulli | © Francesc Guillamet **3** Desu Design **4** Iittala **5, 8** Tools Design **6** Intoto | © Russell Gera **7** Aldo Cibic | © Santi Caleca

Atelier Satyendra Pakhalé | © Frans Feijn

Zwilling J. A. Henckels | © Ursula Raapke

Crack nuts quickly and easily and
decorate your table with these two
attractive wooden cubes.
Casser les noix rapidement et facilement
tout en décorant votre table avec ces
deux jolis cubes en bois.
Mit diesen beiden hübschen Holzwürfeln
kann man Nüsse schnell und einfach
knacken.

Siebensachsen | © Studio Gallandi

Siebensachsen | © Studio Gallandi

Nils Holger Moormar

ls Holger Moormann

This simple, elegant storage system for kitchen utensils consists of panels which are subdivided into individual modules designed for specific uses and to accommodate various objects. The dimensions of the panels follow a specific system to ensure that every individual panel and the number of modules fit together.

Ce simple et élégant système de rangement pour ustensiles de cuisine est constitué de panneaux dotés de protubérances pour accueillir les différents objets subdivisés en modules individuels, conçus pour des utilisations précises. La dimension des panneaux suit un système particulier pour assurer que chaque panneau individuel et le nombre de module aillent ensemble.

Dieses einfache und elegante Lagersystem für Küchenutensilien besteht aus Tafeln, die in verschiedene Module für spezifische Zwecke unterteilt sind, in denen alle möglichen Objekte Platz finden. Die Abmessungen der Tafeln folgen einem spezifischen System, durch das sichergestellt wird, dass jede einzelne Tafel und die Anzahl der Module zueinander passen.

Nils Holger Moormann

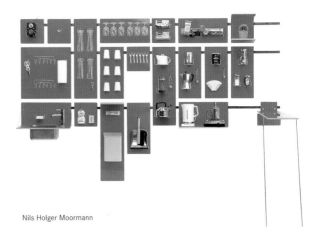

Nils Holger Moormann

Ales

Alessi

Alessi

The mascot created by the designer Stefano Giovannoni for the new Museum of the 21st Century in Taiwan gave birth to the "Family of Mr. Chin" series for the Italian brand A di Alessi. A group of characters are used for this series, each letter representing a specific household function.

La mascotte créée par le designer Stefano Giovannoni pour le nouveau Musée du 21e siècle Century, à Taiwan, a donné naissance à la « Family of Mr. Chin », séries pour l'enseigne italienne A di Alessi. Ces séries utilisent un groupe de caractères, chaque lettre représentant une fonction ménagère spécifique.

Das Maskottchen, das der Designer Stefano Giovannoni für das neue Museum des 21. Jahrhunderts in Taiwan entworfen hat, war der Ursprung für das Entstehen der Serie „Family of Mr. Chin" für die italienische Marke A di Alessi. In dieser Serie werden eine Reihe von Schriftzeichen benutzt, wobei jeder Buchstabe eine spezifische Haushaltsfunktion repräsentiert.

Alessi

Bathroom decoration

Décoration de salle de bains

Badezimmer-Dekoration

Today, thanks to the culture of wellness, the bathroom is enjoying the same esthetic importance as other rooms of the house. The distribution of space and the selection of bathroom fittings are therefore vital, not only for the basic functions these items fulfill but also for the serenity and pleasure they can provide. Here, minimalism is defined by the purity of line and volume of the bathroom furniture and fittings. Washbasins and bathtubs must have the most refined of lines, while taps and other fixtures should display the utmost simplicity in terms of functional items. It is important that personal-care products and cosmetics are kept out of sight in a specific area of the bathroom, whether they are tucked away in compact cabinets or neatly lined up on discreet shelves. Natural-fiber fabrics must be of a single color and pattern-free. Mirrors should be in proportion with furniture tops and their geometric shapes should contribute to the sense of order and relaxing atmosphere of the surroundings.

Agape

Aujourd'hui, la culture du bien-être, élève la salle de bains au même rang esthétique que les autres pièces de la maison. C'est pourquoi, la sérénité et le plaisir qu'elle doit dégager par le biais de la distribution de l'espace et le choix de l'équipement sont aussi importants que ses prestations de base. Le minimalisme se traduit ici par la pureté des volumes de l'équipement. Lavabos et baignoires affichent des lignes épurées avec une robinetterie réduite à des formes simples et fonctionnelles. Les produits d'hygiène et de beauté sont hors de vue, concentrés dans une seule zone de la salle de bains, à l'intérieur d'armoires compactes, ou bien rangées sur des étagères ultra légères. La monochromie est de mise pour les tissus aux couleurs neutres qui n'admettent en aucun cas les imprimés. Les miroirs, quant à eux, respectent les proportions des plans de toilette et agrémentent de leurs formes géométriques un univers régit par l'ordre et la détente.

Da sich in der Gegenwart die Kultur des Wohlbefindens durchgesetzt hat, besitzt das Bad unter ästhetischen Gesichtspunkten heutzutage den gleichen Stellenwert wie andere Räume des Hauses. Deshalb müssen die Schlichtheit und das Wohlbefinden durch die Raumaufteilung erreicht werden. Die Auswahl der Ausstattung ist ebenso wichtig wie die grundlegenden Funktionen. Hier wird der Minimalismus als die Reinheit der Formen der Ausstattungsgegenstände interpretiert. Waschbecken und Badewannen zeigen sich in reinen Linien, die Armaturen sind einfach und funktionell. Die Produkte für die Körperreinigung und Schönheitspflege werden so aufbewahrt, dass man sie nicht sieht, und zwar in einem einzigen Bereich im Bad; entweder in kompakten Schränken oder ordentlich auf leichten Regalen angeordnet. Es herrschen einfarbige Stoffe in Naturfarbe vor. Bedruckte Stoffe sind undenkbar. Die Spiegel passen in ihrer Größe zu den Ablagen und vervollständigen die geometrischen Formen in einer Umgebung, die geordnet und entspannend wirkt.

Toscoquattro

Agape

Muji

Muji

Small bottles and other soap dispensers are not just meant to protect personal-care products. They have become items of decoration in their own right. Transparent containers filled with polychromatic soaps give the bathroom a colorful touch.

Les petits flacons et distributeurs de savon ne font pas que protéger les produits de toilette, mais ils remplissent aussi une fonction décorative. Les récipients transparents peuvent contenir du savon liquide, conférant ainsi au cabinet de toilette un aspect coloré.

Die kleinen Seifenbehälter und -spender dienen nicht nur zum Aufbewahren der Reinigungsprodukte, sondern auch als Dekoration. Transparente Behälter können mit bunter Flüssigseife gefüllt werden und so zu einem Farbtupfer im Badezimmer werden.

Muji

"A place becomes your home when you are sincere."
Ou Baholyodhin

« Un endroit devient votre maison lorsque vous êtes sincère. »
Ou Baholyodhin

„Ein Ort wird zum Zuhause, wenn du aufrichtig bist."
Ou Baholyodhin

1, 4, 5, 7 Toscoquattro 2, 3, 6 © Jordi Sar

Toscoquat

Fine examples of minimalist containers created by the Japanese design firm Muji. As well as being 100 % reusable, transparent recipients with slightly simple shapes can be very attractive.

Cet exemple d'emballage minimaliste vient d'une entreprise de design originaire du Japon, Muji. Les récipients transparents, aux formes simples, sont charmants et en plus recyclables à 100 %.

Ein Beispiel für eine minimalistische Verpackung stammt von dem japanischen Designunternehmen Muji. Die transparenten Behälter, mit klaren Formen, sind nicht nur ein schöner Blickfang, sondern sie können auch zu 100 % wieder verwertet werden.

Armani Casa

rmani Casa

Toscoquattro

"The constant search for the archetypal simplicity should justify, by itself, the birth of a new object in our already over-populated consumer society, without adding gratuitous formal glitz introduced in the project only to please the public."
Alberto Alessi

« La quête constante de la simplicité pour l'art de la simplicité devrait justifier par elle-même la naissance d'un nouvel objet dans notre société de consommation déjà surpeuplée, sans devoir ajouter gratuitement du clinquant formel seulement pour faire plaisir au public. »
Alberto Alessi

„Die ständige Suche nach der archetypischen Einfachheit sollte an sich die Entstehung eines neuen Ziels in unserer überbevölkerten Konsumgesellschaft rechtfertigen, ohne dass man grundlos äußerlichen Glitter in das Projekt aufnehmen muss, um das Publikum zu erfreuen."
Alberto Alessi

Antonio Lupi

Antonio Lup

Today's streamlined plumbing fixtures are compatible with different forms and colors, fulfilling their functions without clashing as decorative elements.
Aujourd'hui, ces robinetteries dépouillées se marient à différentes formes et couleurs, remplissant leurs fonctions sans créer de fausse note sur le plan décoratif.
Die heutigen stromlinienförmigen Armaturen passen zu verschiedenen Formen und Farben und erfüllen so ihre Funktionen, ohne dass sie unangenehm ins Auge fallen.

Estudi Hac

Estudi Hac

Dornbracht

Toscoquattro   Agape Design

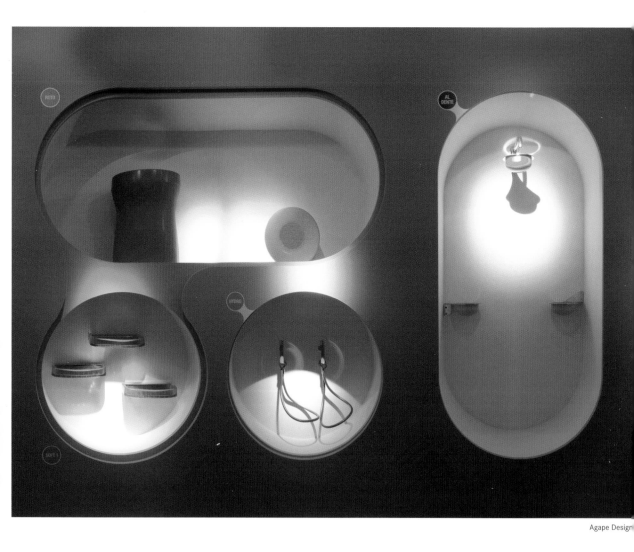

Agape Design

These polyethylene containers give a touch of color to a minimalist bathroom and can be used both as storage equipment and seats thanks to their specially designed lids.

Ces containers en polyéthylène confèrent une touche de couleur à une salle de bains minimaliste. Ils peuvent être utilisés l'un et l'autre comme rangement et se posent aisément grâce à leur couvercle spécialement dessiné à cet effet.

Diese Behälter aus Polyethylen verleihen dem minimalistisch eingerichteten Badezimmer etwas Farbe. Sie können aufgrund ihrer Deckelform sowohl zum Aufbewahren als auch als Hocker benutzt werden.

Agape Design

gape Design

Home decor accessories

Accessoires de décoration d'intérieur

Wohndeko-Zubehör

One of the main rules of minimalism is that 'everything is part of everything', therefore all the elements that are part of the same living space must combine in order to create conceptual unity. If this particular rule is to be applied, all complementary furnishings should appear to be an extension of the main items of furniture and boast the same proportions, albeit in different scales. Accessories such as console tables, small tables, ottomans and footrests play a role that is not merely utilitarian but also vital to the balance of a room. These colorful elements can give warmth to industrial spaces, for instance, or enhance environments dominated by pure white. Different materials can also be used to develop the interaction of their physical characteristics, thus obtaining contrasts such as shiny/matt, smooth/rough or opaque/transparent without breaking the rule of style harmony.

Molteni & C

Selon un des préceptes minimalistes essentiel « tout est partie du tout » et pour cette raison les éléments intégrés dans une même pièce doivent s'associer pour composer une unité conceptuelle. Dans ce sens, les meubles d'appoint s'affichent dans le prolongement de l'équipement central. Cela implique donc – même à différentes échelles – une identité dans les proportions. Les accessoires, tels que guéridons, petites tables, poufs et repose-pieds, jouent un rôle clé dans l'équilibre des pièces, dépassant leur simple fonction utilitaire. Ainsi les espaces industriels peuvent gagner en chaleur par le biais d'accessoires. Quant aux espaces d'une blancheur immaculée absolue, ils peuvent être rehaussés des nuances colorées de ces éléments. L'emploi de matériaux différents permet d'exploiter l'interaction de leurs caractéristiques physiques. C'est ainsi que, selon le principe d'harmonisation de styles, se côtoient des contrastes brillant-mat, doux-rugueux et opaque-transparent.

Eines der wichtigsten Gebote des Minimalismus lautet, dass „alles ein Teil von allem ist". Deshalb müssen die Elemente, die sich in einem Raum befinden, zueinander passen und eine konzeptuelle Einheit bilden. So stellen zum Beispiel Zusatzmöbel eine Erweiterung der zentralen Möbelstücke dar und sollten dabei die gleichen Proportionen, wenn auch in einem anderen Maßstab, haben. Kleinere Einrichtungsgegenstände wie Konsolen, Beistelltische, Puffs und Fußschemel spielen eine Schlüsselrolle für das Gleichgewicht im Raum, das über die reine Funktionalität hinausgeht. So können industrielle Räume mit den entsprechenden Einrichtungsgegenständen wärmer wirken, und in Räumen, in denen ein absolutes Weiß vorherrscht, kann diese Farbe durch Farbnuancen an den Einrichtungsgegenständen noch betont werden. Auch die Verwendung von verschiedenen Materialien ist möglich, um eine Interaktion ihrer physischen Eigenschaften zu ermöglichen. So können, dem Grundsatz der Vereinheitlichung der Stile folgend, Kontraste wie glänzend und matt, weich und rau oder undurchsichtig und durchsichtig miteinander kombiniert werden.

Hjelle

Zanotta

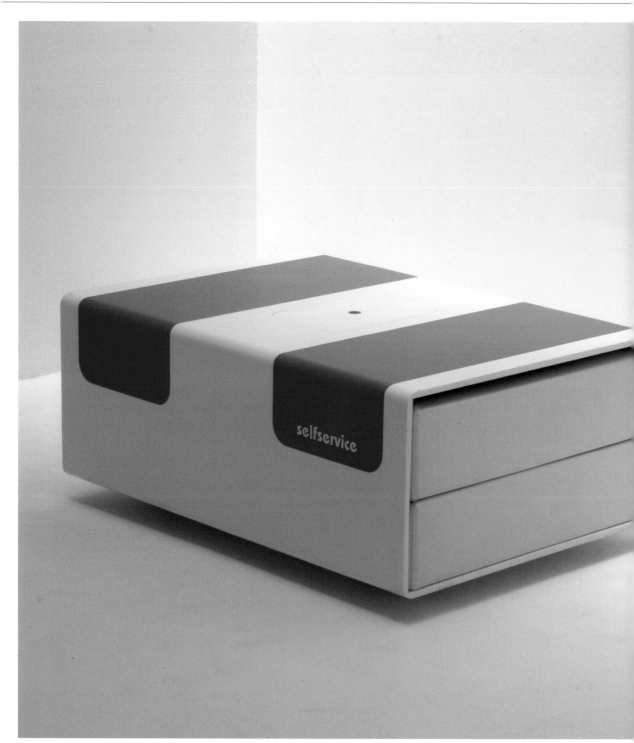

Stone Des

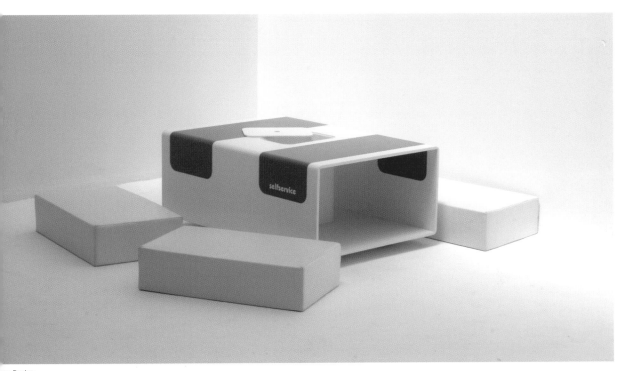

ne Design

Specially designed for small spaces, the self-service table includes four floor cushions to sit on and a central compartment with a lid containing two long tablecloths. With its simple design, this piece gives the room a playful and provocative touch.

Spécialement conçue pour des petits espaces, la table self-service comprend quatre coussins de sol pour s'y asseoir et un compartiment central doté d'un couvercle contenant deux nappes. Grâce à la simplicité de son design, cette oeuvre confère à la pièce une touche à la fois gaie et provocatrice.

Dieser Self-Service-Tisch wurde speziell für kleine Räume entworfen und ist mit vier Kissen bestückt, auf denen man sitzen kann, sowie einem zentralen Element mit Deckel, in dem sich zwei lange Tischtücher befinden. Mit seinem einfachen Design verleiht dieses Element dem Raum einen spielerischen und gewagten Touch.

Desalto

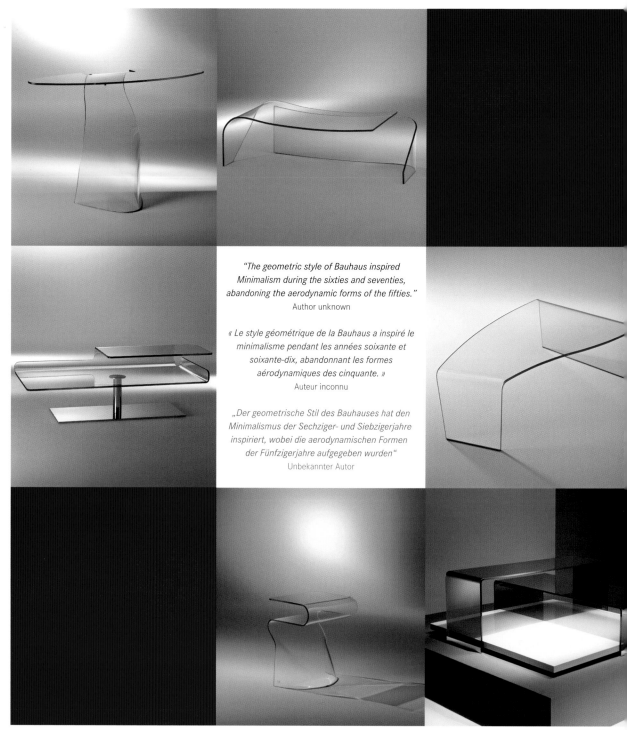

"The geometric style of Bauhaus inspired
Minimalism during the sixties and seventies,
abandoning the aerodynamic forms of the fifties."
Author unknown

« Le style géométrique de la Bauhaus a inspiré le
minimalisme pendant les années soixante et
soixante-dix, abandonnant les formes
aérodynamiques des cinquante. »
Auteur inconnu

„Der geometrische Stil des Bauhauses hat den
Minimalismus der Sechziger- und Siebzigerjahre
inspiriert, wobei die aerodynamischen Formen
der Fünfzigerjahre aufgegeben wurden"
Unbekannter Autor

This sculptured stainless-steel bench is ideal for hallways, galleries and atriums. Despite its massive solidity, it manages to retain its refined minimalist look.
Le banc sculpté en acier inoxydable est idéal pour les couloirs, galeries et atriums. En dépit de sa solidité massive, il parvient à conserver son élégante allure minimaliste.
Diese plastisch wirkende Bank aus Edelstahl eignet sich ausgezeichnet für Korridore, Emporen und Vorhöfe. Trotz ihrer massiven Festigkeit bewahrt die Bank ihr minimalistisches Aussehen.

B&B Italia

B&B Italia

Orange2

Orange22

Orange2

The precision of natural and genuine design combined with the beauty and femininity of nature are the hallmarks of this collection. Each piece consists of a single, precisely cut and shaped piece of aluminum with a high-impact powdered finish or an epoxy-coated wood veneer.

La précision d'un design naturel et franc, associée à la beauté et à la féminité de la nature, telles sont les caractéristiques de cette collection. Chaque pièce est un seul morceau d'aluminium coupé et formé de manière très précise, doté d'une finition poudrée qui fait beaucoup d'effet ou de bois verni revêtu d'époxy.

Die Präzision des ungekünstelten, einfachen Designs mit der Schönheit und der femininen Seite der Natur prägen diese Kollektion. Jedes Element besteht aus einem einzelnen, genau geschnittenen und geformten Aluminiumteil mit einem hochgradig schlagfesten Pulverlack oder einem epoxibeschichtetem Holzfurnier.

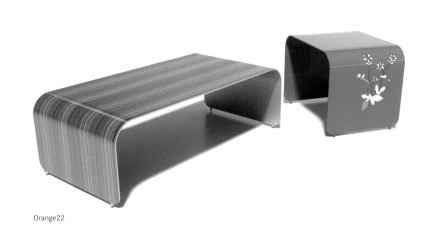

Orange22

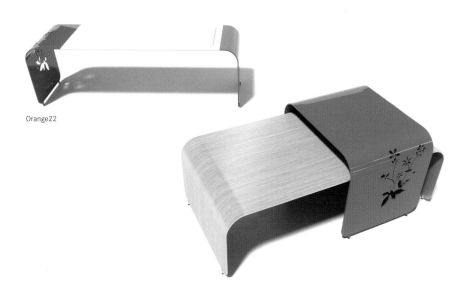

Orange22

Orange22

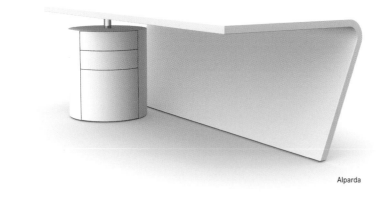

Alparda

Alparda

Downbeat and with endless possible combinations, the Arc Series was designed for modern offices. The simplicity of Aziz Sarıyer's design offers a glimpse of the office of the future where only "necessary" objects will have their place.

Dans l'air du temps et combinable à l'infini, le Arc Series est conçu pour des bureaux modernes. La simplicité du design de Aziz Sarıyer donne un aperçu de ce que peut être le bureau du futur où seuls les objets « nécessaires » ont leur place.

Die „Arc Serie", die unendlich viele Kombinationen zulässt, wurde für das moderne Büro entworfen. Die Einfachheit des Designs von Aziz Sarıyer lässt das Büro der Zukunft erahnen, in dem nur die „notwendigen Objekte" Platz haben werden.

The Moon desk is a versatile, freestanding unit, which can be used as a secretary, a writing desk or a computer table thanks to its convex half-moon shape. The Moon desk won the 2005–2006 Elle Decor International Design Awards (EDIDA).

Le bureau Moon est un module polyvalent et autoportant, qui peut servir de secrétaire, de bureau ou de table pour ordinateur grâce à sa forme de demie lune convexe. Le bureau Moon a reçu, en 2005–2006, le Elle Decor International Design Awards (EDIDA).

Der Tisch „Moon desk" ist eine vielseitige, frei stehende Einheit, die mit ihrer Halbmondform als Sekretär, Schreibtisch oder Computertisch benutzt werden kann. Der „Moon desk" war der Gewinner der „2005–2006 Elle Decor International Design Awards" (EDIDA).

Alparc

dio Arthur Casas

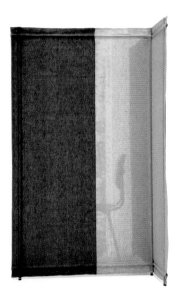

Scholten & Baijings | © Inga Powilleit

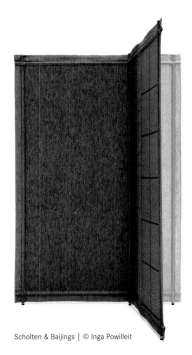

Scholten & Baijings | © Inga Powilleit

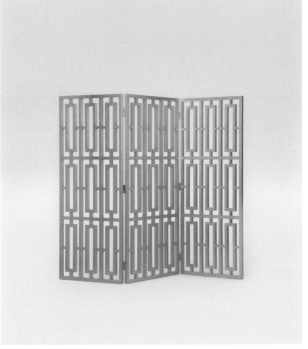

'Still', the three-dimensional fabric wall, creates new relationships between interior living spaces as it can be used as a room divider, a partition system or a screen. The characteristic expressions of its design are transparency, texture, color and the use of patterns. In addition, the interaction of the different layers of fabric and the placement of 'Still' further determine the effect of light and the intensity of color.

« Still », mur en tissu tridimensionnel, crée de nouvelles relations entre les espaces de vie intérieurs car il peut servir de cloison mobile, de système de partition ou de paravent. Transparence, texture, couleur et emploi de motifs sont les expressions caractéristiques de son design. A cela s'ajoutent l'interaction des différentes couches de tissus et le positionnement de « Still », dans l'espace, déterminant l'effet lumineux et l'intensité de couleur.

Die dreidimensionale Textilwand „Still" ermöglicht neue Beziehungen in den Räumen, denn sie kann als Raumteiler, Teilungssystem oder Abschirmung benutzt werden. Transparenz, Textur, Farbe und die Verwendung von Mustern machen das typische Design aus. Durch die Interaktion der verschiedenen Gewebeschichten und die Position von „Still" im Raum kann außerdem die Wirkung der Licht- und Farbintensität gesteuert werden.

Armani Casa

studi Hac

Estudi Hac

This collection of furniture designed by the Spanish design studio Hac is the result of a conception that seeks the projection of light and shadows created on different surfaces. The chairs have simple and pure shapes, while the flowers stand out as distinguished elements.

Cette collection de meubles, signée par le studio de design Hac, est le fruit de l'étude sur la projection de lumières et d'ombres sur différents plans. Les sièges exaltent des formes simples et épurées, alors que les fleurs géométriques se révèlent être des éléments distincts.

Diese Möbelkollektion vom spanischen Designstudio „Hac" ist das Ergebnis der Suche nach Licht und Schatten auf verschiedenen Ebenen. Die Sitze haben einfache, unkomplizierte Formen, auf denen die geometrischen Blumen das charakteristische Element bilden.

Estudi Hac

Estudi Hac

Joan Lao

High-tech design

Design électronique

Elektronik-Design

When designed in accordance with the rules of minimalism, electronic objects acquire a sober, impeccable appearance. Thanks to their design characteristics, they can integrate perfectly into the various spaces where their presence is needed and, far from being the focus of attention, occupy small but strategic positions that make the most of their functions. Minimalist high-tech accessories do not display complex function mechanisms. These remain concealed in simple, compact shapes. Digital equipment with unobtrusive switches, aerials or buttons are the most suitable for a minimalist type of decoration.

Bang & Olufsen

Conçus selon les principes du minimalisme, les objets électroniques adoptent un design impeccable et sobre. Forts de ces caractéristiques, ils s'intègrent facilement à l'espace. Pour ce faire, loin d'être le point de mire, ils occupent un minimum de place, non moins stratégique au moment de déployer leur fonction. Les accessoires technologiques minimalistes se passent d'exhiber des mécanismes de fonctionnement complexes : ils sont plutôt masqués sous des formes simples et compactes. Choisir une décoration minimaliste, c'est recourir à des appareils à fonctionnement numérique, dépourvus d'interrupteurs voyants, d'antennes ou de boutons.

Elektronische Objekte, die nach den Richtlinien des Minimalismus gestaltet sind, zeichnen sich durch ein makelloses und schlichtes Design aus. Aufgrund dieser Gestaltung lassen sich diese Elemente sehr einfach in die Räume integrieren. Deshalb sind sie nicht mehr der Mittelpunkt der Aufmerksamkeit, sondern sie nehmen nur einen kleinen, aber in dem Augenblick, in dem sie ihre Funktion erfüllen sollen, strategisch wichtigen Raum ein. Bei minimalistisch gestalteten, technologischen Geräten hat man auf die Zurschaustellung komplexer Funktionsmechanismen verzichtet. Stattdessen sind diese in einfachen und kompakten Formen verborgen. Wenn man sich für eine minimalistische Raumgestaltung entscheidet, sollte man digitale Geräte ohne auffallende Schalter, Antennen und Tasten wählen.

Suck UK

Bang & Olufsen

Bang & Olufsen

Bang & Olufsen

Bang & Olufsen

Bang & Olufsen

Home Temptation

The passage of time is the concept behind the Dual set of clocks. Depending on the time of day you need to refer to one or perhaps to both clocks to get the full story. A great conversation piece when placed at opposite ends of the mantelpiece or a piece of 'instrumentation' when turned vertically and mounted on the wall.

Le temps qui passe est le concept qui se cache derrière ce double set d'horloges. Selon l'heure du jour, vous devez peut-être vous référez à une ou peut-être deux horloges pour avoir l'heure exacte. Un grand bout de conversation lorsqu'elle est placée à des extrémités opposées sur la cheminée ou un instrument si on le tourne à la verticale ou l'accroche sur le mur.

Das Vergehen der Zeit ist das Konzept, das diesem dualen Uhrenset zugrunde liegt. Je nach der Uhrzeit müssen Sie auf eine oder eventuell auf beide Uhren schauen, um alles zu erfahren. Ein wunderschönes Genrebild, wenn man es auf das entgegengesetzte Ende des Kaminsims stellt oder eine Art Instrument, wenn man es vertikal an die Wand montiert.

Home Temptations

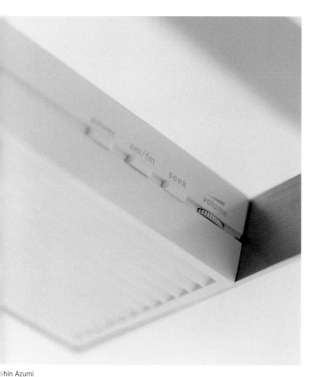

Shin Azumi

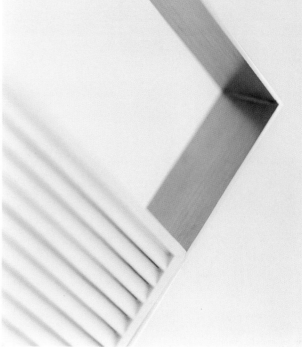

Shin Azumi

Shin Azumi

Launched in the "Open your mind" exhibition in Milan in 2006, this radio was designed using highly technical craftsmanship to evoke the crispness of aluminum.

Inauguré dans l'exposition « Open your mind » à Milan en 2006, le concept de cette radio affiche une facture issue de la technologie de pointe pour évoquer le froissement de l'aluminium.

Dieses Radio, das zum ersten Mal auf der Ausstellung „Open your mind" in Mailand 2006 vorgestellt wurde, ist unter Anwendung bester handwerklicher Kenntnisse gestaltet worden, um die Materialeigenschaft des Aluminiums hervorzuheben.

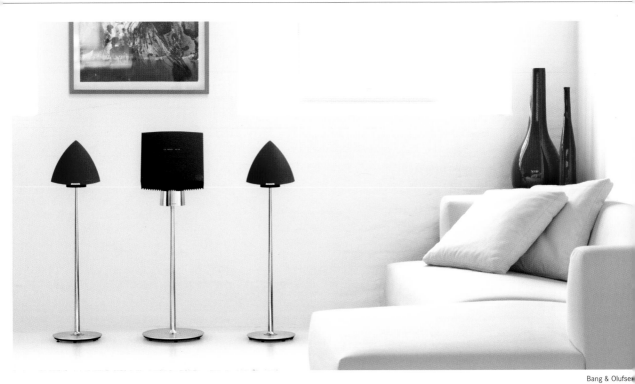

Bang & Olufsen

Bang & Olufsen

Bang & Olufsen

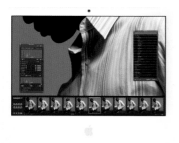

"People are the measurement for all furniture."
Friedrich Wilhelm Möller

« Les gens sont la mesure de tous les meubles. »
Friedrich Wilhelm Möller

„Die Menschen sind das Maß aller Möbel."
Friedrich Wilhelm Möller

1 Artcoustic 2, 4, 5, 6 Apple 3, 7 Hollo

Design Partne

Design Partn

Design Partners

Design Partners

Cubix is a furniture-vending machine.
Simply select the desired piece of
furniture (chair, table, shelf or lamp), pay
for it and take it home. Once there, all
you have to do is pull the ring and in just
a few seconds the chosen product will
unfold before you.

Cubix est une machine à vendre les
meubles. Sélectionner tout simplement le
meuble désiré (chaise, table, étagère ou
lampe), le payer et l'emporter chez soi.
Ensuite, vous n'avez qu'à tirer sur
l'anneau et en quelques secondes le
produit choisi se déplie devant vous.

„Cubix" ist ein Verkaufsautomat für
Möbel. Wählen Sie einfach das
gewünschte Möbelstück (Stuhl, Tisch,
Regal oder Lampe), bezahlen Sie und
nehmen Sie es mit nach Hause. Wenn Sie
zu Hause sind, ziehen Sie an dem Ring
und in ein paar Sekunden entfaltet sich
das gewählte Produkt vor Ihren Augen.

Design Partners

141

Design Partners

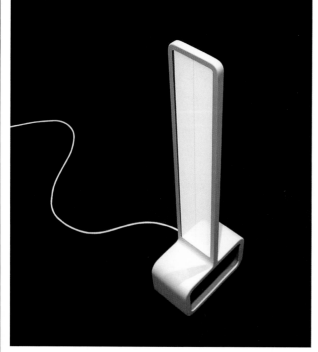

Design Partners

Design Partners

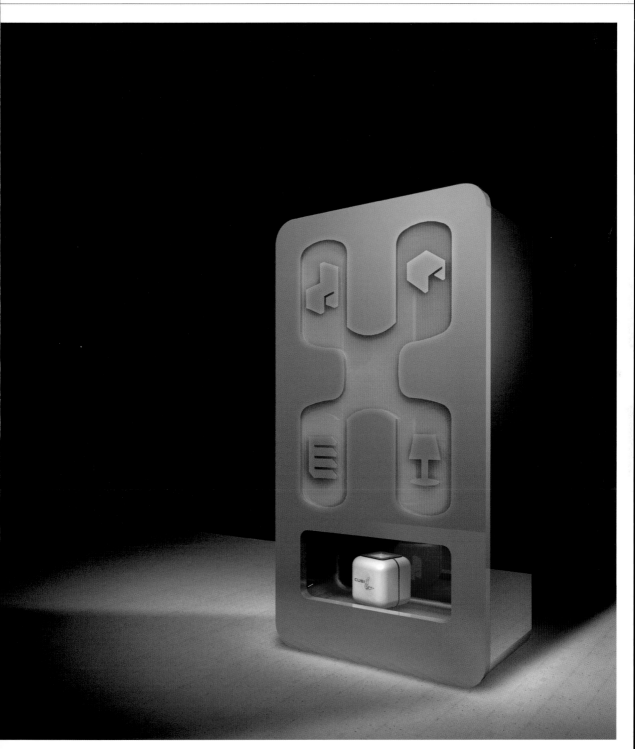

Giulio Oria

Stace Design

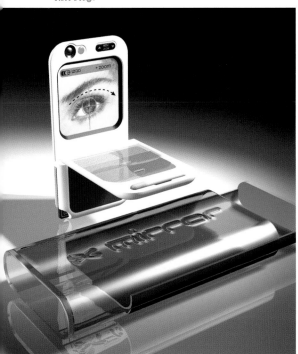

This makeup set includes a video camera and sophisticated software allowing the user to preview various makeup styles. About the size of a mobile phone, its screen is separated from the element by a small tray containing the eyeliner.

Cette boite à maquillage comprend une caméra vidéo et un logiciel sophistiqué permettant à l'utilisateur de passer en revue divers styles de maquillage. De la taille d'un téléphone portable, son écran est séparé de l'élément par un petit plateau contenant un eyeliner.

Dieses Make-up-Set schließt eine Videokamera ein und eine ausgeklügelte Software hilft der Benutzerin, verschiedene Make-up-Stile vorher anzuschauen. Es hat ungefähr die Größe eines Mobiltelefons und der Bildschirm ist von dem Element durch einen kleinen Behälter getrennt, in dem sich der Eyeliner befindet.

ace Design

145

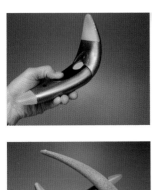

Craig Hin

The Orb is a luminous cellular regenerator that can easily be operated with one hand, just pointing it at the patient's affected area. The most interesting thing about the Orb, however, is that it is not a real medical tool but a fictional prototype for a sci-fi film.

L'Orb est un régénérateur cellulaire lumineux, facilement utilisable d'une main, en le pointant sur la partie malade du patient. Mais ce qui est le plus intéressant, c'est qu'Orb n'est pas un véritable outil médical, mais un prototype de film de science fiction.

Der „Orb" ist ein leuchtender Zellregenerator, der einfach mit einer Hand zu bedienen ist, indem man auf +die betroffene Zone des Patienten zielt. Allerdings ist der „Orb" kein echtes, medizinisches Gerät, sondern ein Prototyp für einen Science-Fiction-Film.

Craig Hines

Bang & Olufsen

Bang & Olufsen   Bang & Olufsen

Natural decoration

Décoration naturelle

Natürliche Dekoration

Inspired by Eastern philosophy, minimalism perceives nature as a representation of the universe that is designed to impart vitality and serenity. Those gardens are perfect for small spaces and require very little upkeep. Their most common components are rocks, gravel, sand, water and, to a limited extent, plants. Ornamentation is left to the natural elements or to neat accessories of natural colors that can integrate harmoniously into the garden. In both cases, ornaments must be distributed in such a way as to leave as much free space as possible. Inside the house, stylized plants of one solid color must be displayed in containers that have pure lines. Vases made of thick transparent glass, for example, can be filled with round pebbles or sand, and are ideal for carrying essential components of a minimalist garden to any part of the house.

© William Dangar

S'inspirant de la philosophie orientale, le minimalisme perçoit la nature comme la représentation de l'univers conçu pour insuffler vitalité et sérénité. Les jardins sont adaptés aux petits espaces et aux besoins d'un jardinage facile. Ils sont fréquemment composés de roches, gravier, sable, eau et de quelques plantes. La décoration met essentiellement en scène des éléments naturels, ou bien, des accessoires aux formes pures et aux couleurs naturelles qui s'intègrent harmonieusement au jardin. Dans les deux cas, l'agencement du décor doit libérer le plus possible l'espace. Dans les intérieurs, les plantes conjuguant allure stylisée et couleurs uniformes sont présentées dans des pots aux formes épurées. Les récipients en verre épais et transparent, idéals pour y mettre des pierres arrondies ou du sable, permettent de transporter dans n'importe quelle partie de la maison les éléments essentiels d'un jardin minimaliste.

Inspiriert von der östlichen Philosophie nimmt der Minimalismus die Natur wie eine Darstellung des Universums wahr, bei der Lebenskraft und Gelassenheit vermittelt werden. Minimalistische Gärten werden auf kleinen Flächen angelegt und sind sehr pflegeleicht. Die üblichen Elemente sind Felsen, Kieselstein, Sand, Wasser und, in kleinerem Maße, Pflanzen. Die schmückenden Elemente sind natürliche Materialien oder Dekorationsgegenstände mit reinen Formen und natürlichen Farben, die sich harmonisch in den Garten einfügen. In beiden Fällen muss man bei der Verteilung dieser schmückenden Elemente so viel freien Platz wie möglich schaffen. In den Räumen finden sich elegant wirkende Pflanzen einheitlicher Farben, die in Blumentöpfen mit reinen Formen stehen. Behälter aus grobem und transparentem Glas werden mit runden Kieselsteinen oder Sand gefüllt, sodass man die grundlegenden Elemente eines minimalistischen Gartens in jeden Teil des Hauses tragen kann.

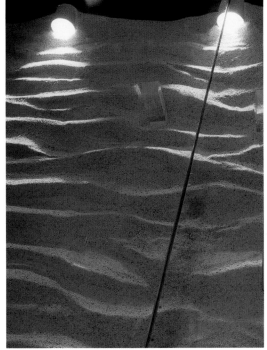

© Jordi Sarrà

© William Dangar

Vitamin

This extraordinary invention combines an ashtray with a flower pot. The pot sits on top of the ashtray, thus concealing it visually and olfactorily.

Cette invention extraordinaire, associe un cendrier à un pot de fleur. Le pot, placé au-dessus du cendrier, est ainsi masqué et les odeurs éliminées.

Diese außergewöhnliche Erfindung ist eine Kombination aus Aschenbecher und Blumentopf. Der Blumentopf befindet sich über dem Aschenbecher, so dass er ihn visuell verbirgt und den Geruch überdeckt.

Vitamin

Bloom!

The main feature of this self-watering plant pot is a medical-drip type of watering system. This unique characteristic allows the plant to receive the right amount of water when it needs it.

La caractéristique principale de ce pot à arrosage automatique est un système d'arrosage de goutte à goutte. Ce système unique permet à la plante de recevoir la quantité exacte d'eau en fonction de ses besoins.

Das Hauptmerkmal dieses sich selbst bewässernden Blumentopfs ist ein Bewässerungssystem, das wie eine Dauertropfinfusion funktioniert. Diese einzigartige Vorrichtung dient dazu, dass die Pflanze stets im richtigen Moment die korrekte Menge an Wasser erhält.

C. Quoi

C. Quoi

This vase is a versatile element that fits together before it spreads out, unfolding its limbs into any desired shape to create an endless extension of flowers.

Ce vase est un élément polyvalent qui s'assemble avant de se démonter, déployant ses cotés sous toutes les formes désirées afin de créer d'infinies compositions florales.

Diese Vase ist ein vielseitiges Element, das sich zuerst zusammenzieht und dann ausbreitet. Ihre Ausläufer nehmen jede gewünschte Form an, um so eine unendliche Verlängerung aus Blumen zu bilden.

Galería Joan Gaspar

*"Light and shade show the poetry of form, just as the folds of a kimono reveal
the hidden positions of the body."*
Author unknown

*« Lumière et ombre révèlent la poésie de la forme, à l'image des plis du kimono
qui découvrent les parties cachées du corps. »*
Autor inconnu

*„Licht und Schatten zeigen die Poesie der Form, so wie die Falten eines
Kimonos die verborgenen Stellen des Körpers zeigen."*
Unbekannter Autor

Ligne Roset

Galería Joan Gaspar

Vitamin

This object is an alternative to the traditional garden gnome. Suitable for both interiors and exteriors, the gnome is at home anywhere, be it near the pond or as a decorative object in the living room.

Cet objet est une alternative au traditionnel nain de jardin. Parfait à l'intérieur comme à l'extérieur, le nain est chez lui partout, que ce soit près de la marre ou comme objet de décor au salon.

Dieses Objekt ist eine Alternative zu dem traditionellen Gartenzwerg. Dieser Zwerg fühlt sich neben einer Brücke im Garten genauso wohl wie als Dekorationsobjekt im Wohnzimmer.

Vitamin

Vitamin

a Maison de Marina

The plant growing through a hole in this heavy, seemingly immovable slab of concrete enhances the structure by allowing it to gradually become part of the landscape.

La plante qui grandit au travers d'un trou, dans ce pot de béton inamovible en apparence, le met en valeur, lui permettant de devenir progressivement un élément du paysage.

Die Pflanze, die aus einer Öffnung dieses schweren, offensichtlich kaum zu bewegenden, Betonblocks herauswächst, lässt ihn allmählich zu einem Teil der Landschaft werden.

a Maison de Marina

Klaus Aalto

Muji

This ready-to-use steel barbecue works with a small gas cartridge which is placed inside the grill. Small enough to carry on the back of a bike, it is perfect for outings.

Ce barbecue en fer, prêt à l'emploi, fonctionne avec une petite cartouche de gaz placée à l'intérieur du grill. Assez compact pour être porté sur un vélo, il est parfait pour les sorties.

Dieser, sofort verwendbare, Stahlgrill funktioniert mit einer kleinen Gaskartusche im Inneren. Er ist so klein, dass man ihn auf einem Fahrrad zum Picknick mitnehmen kann.

Tools Design

C. Quoi

C. Qu

C. Quoi

C. Quo

Dedece

a Oca

Dedece

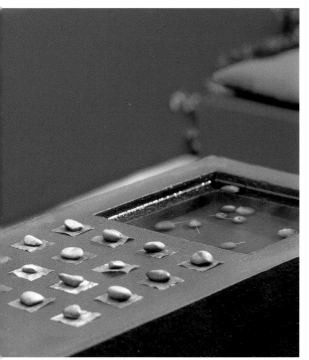

Ben Wrigley

© Taylor Cullity Lethlean

Stones are one of the favorite decorative elements in Japan, where Zen-style gardens, both indoors and outdoors, have been in existence for many centuries.
Les pierres sont un des éléments décoratifs préférés et l'origine de cette fonction vient du Japon. Là, il existe depuis des lustres, ce qu'on appelle les jardins Zen, disposés soit en plein air ou à l'intérieur des maisons.
Steine gehören, dem Beispiel Japans folgend, heute zu den beliebtesten Dekorationselementen. Schon seit Jahrhunderten gibt es die so genannten Zen-Gärten, die sowohl im Freien als auch im Inneren des Hauses angelegt werden.

© Kei Sugino

Decorative complements

Eléments décoratifs complémentaires

Dekorations-Zubehör

Minimalist decoration contains very few objects. The pieces chosen should have geometrical and stylized lines and, following the maxim "less is more", be of a medium-to-large size. If they are meant to be centerpieces, the best place for them are clear, open spaces and smooth surfaces. If the objects displayed in the same environment are part of a balanced scheme, the rules of repetition and symmetry must be obeyed. In a universe governed by order, superpositions are forbidden. To create a harmonious environment, only tones directly inspired by nature—from transparencies to gray and black, or even the whole range of whites—must be used in the decoration. Dashes of intense colors are acceptable in objects with pure lines and without ornaments.

Molteni & C

La décoration minimaliste se compose d'un minimum d'objets, aux lignes géométriques et stylisées. Respectant le principe « moins c'est plus », elle a recours à des pièces de taille moyenne ou plus grandes, qui, placées dans des zones dépouillées aux surfaces lisses, se transforment en points de mire. La distribution de ces objets au sein d'une même ambiance doit correspondre à un schéma équilibré. Il y a donc des règles à suivre, comme la répétition et la symétrie. Dans cet univers où l'ordre est roi, les superpositions sont interdites. Pour créer l'harmonie avec l'environnement, la décoration n'utilise qu'une palette de teintes inspirées directement de la nature, partant des transparences, en passant par le gris et le noir, jusqu'au blanc dans toute sa gamme. Mais il est tout de même permis d'avoir quelques touches de couleurs intenses sur des objets aux lignes pures dépourvus de décor.

Die minimalistische Dekoration besteht aus sehr wenigen Objekten mit geometrischen und stilisierten Linien. In Anlehnung an den Leitsatz „Weniger ist mehr" benutzt man mittelgroße oder große Elemente, die in offenen Bereichen mit glatten Flächen aufgestellt werden und so den Raum beherrschen. Diese Objekte müssen gleichmäßig innerhalb des Raumes verteilt werden. Man kann dazu Regeln, wie die der Wiederholung oder der Symmetrie, befolgen. In diesem Universum, in dem die Ordnung herrscht, sind Überlagerungen verboten. Um Harmonie im Raum zu schaffen, sollte man für die Dekoration nur Farbtöne benutzen, die direkt von der Natur inspiriert sind; angefangen bei den Transparenzen, über Grau und Schwarz bis hin zu Weiß in all seinen Nuancen. Auch kleine Farbtupfer sind zulässig, wenn sie an Objekten mit reinen Linien ohne Verzierungen zu finden sind.

Desu Design

Dedece

Koziol

Koz

Inspired by the Japanese cherry blossom, this element works best in vertical installations and is ideal as a wall covering or an airy room divider. The pieces are simply hooked together and can be bent or shaped any which way.

Inspiré de la floraison du cerisier, cet élément est du plus bel effet lorsqu'il est installé à la verticale. Il est idéal comme revêtement mural ou comme paravent léger et transparent. Les morceaux sont tout simplement accrochés ensemble et peuvent être formés ou tordus de diverses façons à souhait.

Dieses, von der japanischen Kirschblüte inspirierte, Element eignet sich ausgezeichnet für vertikale Konstruktionen und bildet eine ideale Wandverkleidung oder einen luftigen Raumteiler. Die Teile werden einfach zusammengesteckt und können in alle Richtungen gebogen und geformt werden.

Koziol

Nahar

La Oca

La Oc

Estudi Hac

Steven Haulenbeek

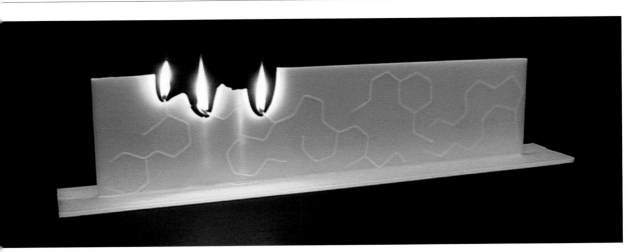

Dedece

Dedece   Dedece

The design of these simple and elegant candles was based on the careful study of the intrinsic qualities of candles as everyday objects. Those very qualities define the product and give it its authenticity, thus establishing a contemporary style that is both alive and genuine.

Le design de ces bougies simples et élégantes repose sur l'étude précise des qualités intrinsèques des bougies comme objets quotidiens. Ces qualités précises définissent le produit et lui confèrent son authenticité, tout en établissant un style contemporain, à la fois vivant et original.

Das Design dieser einfachen und eleganten Kerzen basiert auf einer sorgfältigen Analyse der wesentlichen Eigenschaften von Kerzen als Alltagsobjekten. Diese Eigenschaften definieren das Produkt und machen es originell. So entsteht ein zeitgemäßer Stil, der gleichzeitig lebendig und authentisch wirkt.

Dedece

Joan Lao

*"One explanation for the richness of simplicity might be that an architecture
that refers to nothing outside itself and makes no appeal to the intellect,
automatically prioritizes experience, the sensory experience of space,
material and light."*
Hans Ibelings

*« Une explication à la richesse de la simplicité pourrait être que
l'architecture qui ne se réfère à rien d'autre en dehors d'elle-même, qui
n'interpelle pas l'intellect, laisse automatiquement la priorité à l'expérience
directe, l'expérience sensorielle de l'espace matière et lumière. »*
Hans Ibelings

*„Eine Erklärung des Reichtums der Einfachheit könnte es sein, dass die
Architektur, die sich nicht auf etwas außerhalb ihrer selbst bezieht, die nicht
den Verstand anspricht, automatisch der direkten Erfahrung den Vorzug
gibt, der sinnlichen Wahrnehmung des Raums, des Materials und des
Lichts."*
Hans Ibelings

Joan Lao

"Cultural evolution is equivalent to the removal
of ornament from articles in daily use."
Adolf Loos

« L'évolution culturelle, c'est éliminer les décors
de tous les articles au quotidien. »
Adolf Loos

„Die kulturelle Entwicklung entspricht der
Abschaffung des Ornaments in allen
Gebrauchsgegenständen."
Adolf Loos

Molteni & C

Armani Casa

Armani Casa

Armani Casa

Candles are an essential component of minimalist decoration as they create a relaxed, contemplative atmosphere by diffusing a pleasant, welcoming light in every room.

Les bougies sont créatrices d'ambiance et constituent un élément inséparable de la décoration minimaliste. Elles créent une atmosphère relaxante et de méditation, enveloppant chacune des pièces d'une lumière agréable et accueillante.

Kerzen sorgen für Atmosphäre und sind ein unentbehrliches Element der minimalistischen Dekoration. Sie schaffen eine entspannende und meditative Stimmung und spenden ein angenehmes und einladendes Licht in den Räumen.

Armani Casa

Armani Casa

© Jordi Sarrà

© Jordi Sarrà

© Jordi Sarrà

cher Bobois

Joan La

© Jordi Sarrà

Slightly larger than average dinner plates, these wooden ones fit in perfectly with a discreet and simple style of table decoration.
Légèrement plus grandes que les assiettes à dîner habituelles, ces plats en bois sont parfaits pour un style de décoration discret et simple.
Diese hölzernen Teller sind etwas größer als die üblichen Essteller. Sie passen ausgezeichnet zu einem diskret und einfach dekorierten Esstisch.

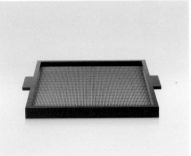

Armani Casa

Armani Casa

Armani Casa

Agape Design
Via Po Barna, 69
46031 Correggio Micheli di
Bagnolo San Vito (MN)
Italy
www.agapedesign.it

Aldo Cibic/Cibic & Partners
Via Varese, 18
20121 Milano
Italy
www.cibicpartners.com

Alessi
Via Privata Alessi, 6
28887 Crusinallo di Omegna (VB)
Italy
www.alessi.com

Alparda
Showroom Office Furniture
Reflit Galip Cad., 87
06700 G.O.P. Ankara
Turkey
www.alparda.com

Amor de Madre
Bilbao, 6
08800 Vilanova i la Geltrú, Barcelona
Spain
www.amordemadre.com

Antonio Lupi Design
Via Mazzini, 73-75
50050 Stabbia
Cerreto Guidi (FI)
Italy
www.antoniolupi.it

Apple
1 Infinite Loop
Cupertino, CA 95014
USA
www.apple.com

Armani Casa
Via Manzoni, 37
20121 Milano
Italy
www.armanicasa.com

Arper
Via Lombardia, 16
31050 Monastier (TV)
Italy
www.arper.it

Atelier Satyendra Pakhalé
Zeeburgerpad, 50
1019 AB Amsterdam
The Netherlands
www.satyendra-pakhale.com

Balvi
Av. Baix LLobregat, 9-11 P. I. Mas Blau II
08820 El Prat de LLobregat, Barcelona
Spain
www.balvi.com

Bang & Olufsen
Peter Bangs Vej, 15
7600 Struer
Denmark
www.bang-olufsen.com

B&B Italia
Strada provinciale, 32
22060 Novedrate (CO)
Italy
www.bebitalia.it

Bellato International
Via Brigata Marche, 2/a
31036 Istrana (TV)
Italy
www.bellato.com

Biosca & Botey
Rambla de Catalunya, 129, 4º
08008 Barcelona
Spain
www.bioscabotey.com

Bloom
25 The Village
101 Amies Street
London, SW11 2JW
United Kingdom
www.bloom-design.com

Bonaldo
Via Straelle, 3
35010 Villanova (PD)
Italy
www.bonaldo.it

Büro für Form
Bereiteranger, 15
81541 Munich
Germany
www.buerofuerform.de

C. Quoi
Pierre & Véronique de Laubadère
254, rue des Ormeaux
44521 Oudon
France
www.c-quoi.com

Casamania
Via S. Elena, 3
31040 Signoressa di Trevignano (TV)
Italy
www.casamania.it

Craig Hines Design
10 Miller Place Suite 1701
San Francisco, CA 94108
USA
www.craighinesdesigns.com

Dedece
263 Liverpool Street
2010 Darlinghurst, Sydney
Australia
www.dedece.com

Desalto
Via per Montesolaro
22063 Cantù (CO)
Italy
www.desalto.it

Design Partners
IDA Business Park
Southern Cross Route
Bray Co. Wicklow
Ireland
www.designpartners.ie

Desu Design
87 Richardson St.
Brooklyn, NY 11211
USA
www.desudesign.com

Droog Design
Staalstraat, 7a
1011 JJ Amsterdam
The Netherlands
www.droogdesign.nl

El Bulli
Cala Montjoi, Ap. 30
17480 Roses, Girona
Spain
www.elbulli.com

Enric Rovira
Sant Geroni, 17
08296 Castellbell i El Vilar
Spain
www.enricrovira.com

Estudi Hac
Paseo Germanías, 12 bajo dcha.
46870 Ontinyent, Valencia
Spain
www.estudihac.com

Fiam Italia
Via Ancona
61010 Tavullia (PU)
Italy
www.fiamitalia.it

Galería Joan Gaspar
Pza. Dr. Letamendi, 1
08007 Barcelona
Spain
www.galeriajoangaspar.com

Georg Jensen Public
Søndre Fasanvej, 7
2000 Frederiksberg
Denmark
www.georgjensen.com

Hjelle
Vik
6230 Sykkylven
Norway
www.hjelle.no

Home Temptations
Saxon Way Industrial Estate
Melbourn, Hertfordshire SG8 6DN
Australia
www.hometemptations.com

Iittala
Hämeentie 135
P.O. Box 130
00561 Helsinki
Finland
www.iittala.com

IKEA
Plaza del Comercio s/n
28700 San Sebastián de los Reyes, Madrid
Spain

Intoto
10 Liberty Street 36
New York, NY 10005
USA
www.intotonyc.com

Jakob Timpe
Prinzenstr. 39
10969 Berlin
Germany
www.jakobtimpe.com

Joan Lao
Rosellon, 214
08008 Barcelona
Spain
www.joanlao.com

Joseph Gracetta & Dario Buzzini
IDEO
630 Davis Street
Evanston, IL 60201
USA

Julian Appelius
Schönhauser Allee 182
0119 Berlin
Germany
www.julianappelius.de

Klaus Aalto
Punavuorenkatu 20 E 47
00150 Helsinki
Finland
www.imudesign.org

Koziol
Werner-von-Siemens-Str.90
64711 Erbach/Odenwald
Germany
www.koziol.de

La Maison de Marina
1 rue d'Andenne
1060 Brussels
Belgium
www.lamaisondemarina.com

La Oca
Paseo Independencia, 19, 6.ª dcha.
50001 Zaragoza
Spain
www.laoca.com

Ligne Roset
Industriestraße, 51
79194 Gundelfingen/Freiburg
Germany
www.ligne-roset.de

Lievore Altherr Molina
Pza. Ramon Berenguer el Gran, ático
08002 Barcelona
Spain
www.lievorealtherrmolina.com

Marset Iluminación
Alfonso XII, 429-431
08918 Barcelona
Spain
www.marset.com

Molteni & C
Via Rossini, 50
20034 Giussano (MI)
Italy
ww.molteni.it

Muji Spain
Rambla Catalunya, 81
08008 Barcelona
Spain
www.muji.co.uk

Müller Möbelfabrikation
Werner-von-Siemens-Str. 6
86159 Augsburg
Germany
www.mueller-moebel.com

Naharro
Granada, 57
28007 Madrid
Spain
www.naharro.com

Nanimarquina
Església, 10, 3 D
08024 Barcelona
Spain
www.nanimarquina.com

Nils Holger Moormann
An der Festhalle, 2
D-83229 Aschau im Chiemgau
Germany
www.moormann.de

Orange22
125 West 4th Street
Studio 102
Los Angeles, CA 90013
USA
www.orange22.com

Pallucco
Via Azzi, 36
31040 Castagnole di Paese (TV)
Italy
www.pallucco.net

Performa möbel und design gmbh
Marbacher straße, 54
74385 Pleidelsheim
Germany
www.performa.de

Rocher Bobois
18, rue de Lyon - 52 et 54
Avenue Ledru Rollin, 75012 Paris
France
www.rochebobois.com

Santa & Cole
Parc de Belloch, Ctra. C-251, Km 5,6
08430 La Roca del Vallès, Barcelona
Spain
www.santacole.com

Schiffini
Via Genova, 206
19020 Ceparana (SP)
Italy
www.schiffini.it

Scholten & Baijings
Sandvikweg 2-B
1013 BA Amsterdam
The Netherlands
www.scholtenbaijings.com

Sellex
Arretxe Ugalde, Ezurriki Kalea 8-10
20305 Irun, Guipuscoa
Spain
www.sellex.es

Shin Azumi
12A Vicars Road
London NW5 4NL
United Kingdom
www.shinazumi.com

Stace Design
Corso Vercelli, 14
20145 Milano
www.stace.it

Steven Haulenbeek
1720 N. Hermitage Ave.
Chicago, IL 60622
USA
www.stevenhaulenbeek.com

Stone Design
Cordón, 10
28005 Madrid
Spain
www.stone-dsgns.com

Stua
Polígono 26
20115 Astigarraga, San Sebastián
Spain
www.stua.com

Studio Arthur Casas
Rua Capivari, 160
Sao Paulo, 01246-020
Brazil
www.arthurcasas.com.br

Suck UK Ltd
8 Andrews Rd
London, E8 4QN
United Kingdom
www.suck.uk.com

Tom Dixon
4 Northington Street
London, WC1N 2JG
United Kingdom
www.tomdixon.net

Tools Design
Rentemestervej 23A
2400 Copenhagen NV
Denmark
www.toolsdesign.dk

Toscoquattro
Via Sila, 40
59100 Prato
Italy
www.toscoquattro.it

Vitamin
The Old Truman Brewery
91 Brick Lane
London, E1 6QL
United Kingdom
www.vitamindesign.co.uk

Vitra
Charles-Eames-Strasse 2
79576 Weil am Rhein
Germany
www.vitra.com

Zanotta
Via Vittorio Veneto, 57
20054 Nova Milanese
Italy
www.zanotta.it

Zwilling J. A. Henckels
Grünewalder Strasse 14-22
42657 Solingen
Germany
www.zwilling.com